Praise for *The Shakedown*

Any system that lacks mutual accountability becomes one-sided in a hurry. To most, "America" means a fair playing field, with reasonable justice, clear laws and balanced enforcement. This vision sits well sideways from a system where "enforcers" act without recourse, can be badly, horribly wrong, yet bear no threat of penalty or demotion. When our own government—personified through its agents and employees—applies its limitless resources, who can stand in its way? *The Shakedown* shows how "being wrong" has no more meaning to an over-zealous prosecutor than destroying a businessman, taking away his livelihood and hope, and beating the "little guy" to a pulp. Who cares? Apparently, only the little guy.

 —Cliff Roesler
  Managing Director
  Angle Advisors, LLC

Meticulously researched but highly-readable, *The Shakedown* shows how unaccountable federal prosecutors routinely misuse their broad powers to manufacture evidence, coerce testimony, and prejudice juries in order to win cases. This is a great read for anyone who truly wants to know how the justice system actually functions, and why this could happen to you!

 —Scott Dantuma
  Turnaround Consultant

I have been on both sides of the law enforcement fence and can tell you this case never would have been prosecuted in the Northern District of Illinois.

> —Dennis E. Czurylo, Principal / Member,
> Dennis E. Czurylo & Associates, LLC.
> Certified Fraud Examiner & Enrolled Agent
> Former IRS Special Agent, U. S. Treasury
> Department

The true story of what Steven Whiting went through and the resources that the federal government devoted to this vendetta are both shocking and scary. We should all be concerned—if it can happen to Whiting under these circumstances, can it happen to us?

> —Christopher Sackett
> Business Attorney

THE SHAKEDOWN

THE SHOCKING TRUE STORY OF THE EXTORTION
AND WRONGFUL PROSECUTION OF AN ENTREPRENEUR–
AND THE TRUTH ABOUT THE FEDERAL CRIMINAL
JUSTICE SYSTEM, EMPLOYEES' UNIONS AND THE
DEMONIZATION OF AMERICAN BUSINESS

STEVEN E. WHITING

FRANKLIN PRESS, LLC.

FRANKLIN PRESS, LLC.

Franklin Press, LLC.
544 East Ogden Avenue
Suite 700
Milwaukee, Wisconsin 53202
www.FranklinPressLLC.com

First Printing: October 2012

Publisher's Cataloging-in-Publication
Whiting, Steven E.
The shakedown: the shocking true story of the extortion and wrongful prosecution of an entrepreneur: and the truth about the federal criminal justice system, employees' unions and the demonization of American business/Steven E. Whiting.
p. cm.
Includes bibliographical references and index.
LCCN 2012934649
ISBN 978-0-9850333-0-9
1. Whiting, Steven E. 2. Businesspeople—United States—Biography.
3. Entrepreneurship—United States. 4. Malicious prosecution—United States.
I. Title.
HC102.5.W45A3 2012   338'.04'092
QBI12-600066

Edited by: Carrie Cantor
Cover and interior design: 1106 Design

Printed in the United States of America on acid-free paper

Dedication

This book is dedicated to all the thousands of innocent individuals who are both still incarcerated and who had been released. Their sacrifices are many.

Acknowledgments

First and foremost, I would like to thank my wife, Marie, who has had to put up with the stress of my legal battles, indictment, incarceration and herself being threatened by a federal prosecutor in his attempt to coerce me. Not to mention all of the eight-hour driving trips she took to visit me while I was incarcerated in Duluth, Minnesota. I would like to thank my friends, family and business associates who stuck by my side during this whole ordeal and encourage me to fight on—a fight that continues to this very day. I would also like to thank my editor, Carrie Cantor, who helped me develop this manuscript all the way from concept to the final line-edit, a project I thought would never get done.

Contents

PART TWO—A SERIOUSLY FLAWED JUDICIAL SYSTEM

Preface

ON FRIDAY, FEBRUARY 4, 2005, my attorney, Michael
Fitzgerald, sent me an email that said the following:

> I have had additional discussions with the U.S.
> Attorney's office. The offer on the table is: (a) put
> $400,000 in an escrow account (b) plead to one count
> with a five-year maximum (c) joint recommendation
> of a year and a day. The deadline for accepting this
> is 5 p.m. Monday.

For nearly three years, I had been up to my eyeballs in civil
litigation stemming from the botched sale of my company, Badger
Die Casting. Although the buyer of Badger, as a matter of law, was
responsible for all outstanding employee benefits, he had failed
to pay those benefits—namely $400,000 in healthcare claims.
Yet, the employee's union had chosen to sue *me*, most likely to
avoid jeopardizing its contract negotiations with the new owner.

Whatever their reason, the union instigated several forms of
litigation in its effort to get me to pay up, including a National
Labor Board complaint; two federal civil lawsuits by the
Department of Labor (DOL); a state civil lawsuit from the
Wisconsin Department of Justice; and the union's own federal

lawsuit. Not only was I defending myself against all of these suits, I was also suing both the purchaser of Badger and the bank that had orchestrated the sale in what my attorneys alleged to be a breach of contract, conspiracy, breach of fiduciary duty, and aiding and abetting.

In the meantime, perhaps because they were not winning any of the civil cases, union officials pursued other avenues and found an ally in the U.S. Attorney's office. As a result, I was charged in a thirteen-count federal criminal indictment alleging that I had intentionally misused $72,878 of employee payroll deductions intended for my company's ERISA plans.

Many aspects of all of this just weren't right. I had not been involved in employee payroll deductions and had not committed any crime. And the amount my company supposedly owed was relatively small, the type of sum normally handled by the Department of Labor as a civil matter. In fact, two DOL civil lawsuits had already been filed against me involving the same $72,878.

Nevertheless, after I received the details of the government's plea offer several months later, it all started to make sense. The federal prosecutor required that I plead guilty to one count and place $400,000 in escrow to be used to settle the union's lawsuit over the healthcare claims. Surprisingly, there was no condition from the government that I pay the $72,878 for which I had been criminally charged in the first place.

It finally dawned on me: this whole criminal matter was a shakedown organized by the federal prosecutor on behalf of the union, at taxpayer expense.

I did not take the prosecutor's so-called deal. And that decision led to a trial, my incarceration, an extensive appeal, and finally a habeas corpus petition pending before the court as of this writing. All of this legal nonsense has already cost taxpayers perhaps well over $1 million.

During this ordeal, I learned an enormous lesson on just how federal prosecutors, using their considerable unchecked power, routinely abuse our criminal justice system to pursue ends other than justice. I hope you will find my true story both shocking and compelling.

Introduction

I HAVE BEEN AN ENTREPRENEUR for thirty years. I started in the insurance and investment business at the age of twenty-four and then, some twenty years later, came to own and operate several multimillion-dollar corporations. During my career, I found working with companies experiencing financial difficulties to be not only the most interesting, but also the most challenging of all my business endeavors. To get my hands on a business that was only a few days away from extinction and reshape it into one that was thriving was not only financially rewarding, but also provided me with the sense that I was making a difference by helping people remain employed and serving our economy.

I eventually worked with over two hundred different troubled companies as a business consultant helping most of them survive and stay in business. I went on to purchase, own, and operate more than fifteen different businesses, from startups to existing companies that were financially distressed.

I learned early on in my consulting career that business owners take on tremendous personal financial risk. I also found this out by having to personally guarantee the debt of many of the companies that I owned and operated, amounting to millions of dollars of potential liability. Yet, putting all my family's financial net worth on the line to own these companies was something I was willing to do. Little did I know there would be hazards in business ownership much greater than the risks I had anticipated. As a law-abiding citizen, I never realized that I was actually risking my personal liberty and freedom!

After several years of consulting and purchasing distressed businesses, I started to acquire larger and more challenging troubled companies. Between 1997 and 2001, I purchased four such companies. In fact, the acquisition in 2001 was my fifteenth acquisition since 1989. These four manufacturing businesses had almost four hundred employees and revenues of more than $107 million over the preceding forty-eight months. I paid out over $44 million in employee wages, benefits, and taxes. I also had business assets of $20 million and a company employee 401(k) plan with approximately $2 million in value.

By the end of 2002, three of my companies had been sold. One of them, Badger Die Casting, had been sold by the bank in what turned out to be an unapproved and disputed sale to an individual who happened to be one of Badger's senior employees at the time. This sale was completed without my approval or consent in what my attorneys alleged to be a conspiracy resulting in a deceptive and fraudulent transfer by the bank.

The consequence of this bank-guided sale was that all assets and cash were removed from Badger, creating a situation in which employee benefits could not be paid. Needless to say, massive and protracted litigation ensued between the buyer of Badger, the bank, the employees' union, and myself. To make matters worse, the Department of Labor started an inquiry into the unpaid Badger employee benefits, resulting in a criminal investigation that viewed me as the only apparent target.

As it turned out, federal prosecutors convinced a grand jury to return a thirteen-count indictment charging me with deliberately misusing $72,878 in employee payroll deductions and making several false statements involving our healthcare plan. In fact, I had no way of knowing whether the government's allegations were true, since employee payroll and deductions were administered by each company's controller and their respective accounting departments, and if these employee deductions had not been paid out, it was clearly an oversight and nobody's fault.

I rejected the government's plea offer and in May 2005 proceeded to trial. After a weeklong jury trial, I was, to my surprise, convicted of ten counts: eight counts that I intentionally converted $37,156.23 in employee payroll deductions and two counts that I knowingly made false statements. I was acquitted of three counts. Needless to say, my family and I were shocked and devastated, but we all continued to believe that this conviction would be overturned during my appeal. In February 2006, I was sentenced to ninety months in federal prison. In December 2006, I won part of my appeal in the Seventh Circuit Court and was resentenced to forty months, of which I served around thirty months.

While there are many troubling aspects of my case (I won't be discussing the toll this process took on my family, friends, and career), the most profound is that the prosecutor, Gordon P. Giampietro, spent perhaps $1 million of taxpayer money in prosecuting this matter for what turned out to be a sum of $37,156.23, a case that could have been quickly and easily resolved as a civil matter.

Justice is about finding the truth, but as you will learn in this book that is not always what happens when federal prosecutors investigate a case. Most people believe that before a federal prosecutor decides to seek criminal charges against someone, the prosecutor has thoroughly investigated the issues surrounding the person's conduct and has determined that a crime has actually been committed. I am sure there are many decent, ethical federal prosecutors who work for our country every day making sure justice is properly administered, who weigh the evidence and make reasonable decisions based on the truth. But there are way too many unscrupulous prosecutors who just want to win cases, even if justice is not served. When such prosecutors decide to go after someone who is innocent and does not plead out, they often manipulate the system to make it appear that a crime actually happened. They are masters of illusion. They work their magic by misleading the court, manipulating witnesses, creating and presenting false evidence to the jury, and making false arguments to jurors unsupported by the evidence.

Why does this happen? For many reasons. It may be that the prosecutor personally does not like the individual who is the subject of the investigation; the prosecutor may want to help someone who has a financial interest in the outcome of the prosecution; or the prosecutor may want to advance his or her career by gaining a reputation as tough and effective. Whatever the prosecutor's motivation, it is often not what it should be, which is to administer justice.

You might wonder how a prosecutor can get away with such illegal conduct. It's actually quite simple. The Supreme Court has mandated that federal prosecutors are protected from civil lawsuits even when it's proven that they manufactured false evidence and suborned perjury and used this evidence at trial to convict an innocent person. The only remaining remedy against such a prosecutor is the Office of Professional Responsibility (OPR), an agency within the Department of Justice (DOJ)—the prosecutor's employer. But according to a *USA Today* report, more than two hundred cases involving misconduct by federal prosecutors that were reported to the OPR resulted in *not one* prosecutor ever being fired. Instead, the DOJ often classifies prosecutors' misconduct as just a mistake.

Consequently, the dishonest federal prosecutor can manufacture evidence, cause witnesses to lie during their testimony, and mislead the jury, with complete confidence that he or she will be protected from both civil rights lawsuits and loss of their employment with the DOJ.

I hope my personal story and analysis of how our legal processes works will convey just how dangerous our federal criminal justice system has become for the innocent business person who might one day might find himself or herself targeted by some overzealous federal prosecutor without any real protection or recourse. Perhaps this book will provoke discussion and inspire efforts to institute laws to better protect the innocent business person and punish federal prosecutors who believe they are above the law, who violate the constitutional rights we all possess in this great country of ours. The type of so-called justice that I experienced erodes the integrity of our system and public confidence in the very government charged with protecting the rights of its citizen.

Part One

MY STORY

Chapter 1

A Serial Entrepreneur

GROWING UP, I was always a bit of a risk-taker. I learned at an early age that to achieve something I had to be willing to take chances. This outlook on life and philosophy served me well over the years, from getting my pilot's training at the age of seventeen to later running several businesses. I prided myself on knowing how to assess risks, set goals, and get things done.

My dad was a lifelong employee of IBM and my mom managed a home that also included my sister, two brothers, and several dogs. As part of a family that relocated quite often due to my father's career, I viewed each move as an opportunity to learn new things, make new friends, and gain an appreciation for the world around me.

After completing my studies in business administration at the University of Wisconsin, I started my business career at the age of twenty-four in the insurance and investment business. I had many years of success, but eventually discovered I wanted to get into the business of acquiring companies. After spending quite some time researching the industry and its methods, I quickly concluded that acquiring troubled businesses, turning them around, and reselling them would be potentially more profitable than acquiring companies that were already doing well. I became determined to learn how to fix such companies.

I hooked up with a firm out of Chicago that provided turn-around-consulting services to troubled companies. In particular, they specialized in saving businesses destined for failure due to substantial debt loads that they could not support. The firm's expertise was in "balance-sheet turnarounds" in what was called "alternatives to bankruptcy." One of the firm's principals, the late Arnold Goldstein, a bankruptcy attorney, professor, and prolific author, determined early on that for many businesses, bankruptcy, with its extremely low success rate, was a waste of time.

I eventually worked with this firm and was trained to fix troubled businesses without the use of bankruptcy. In time, I opened my own consulting practice providing these services to businesses in Wisconsin and other parts of the Midwest.

Consulting to Troubled Companies

I established my consulting company as the Garrett Group in 1990 and opened up an office in Franklin, Wisconsin. There I met with many small-business owners who were experiencing substantial financial problems and were on the brink of going under. These problems involved bank defaults, unpaid payroll and sales taxes, lawsuits, judgments, legal attachments and execution, unsecured creditor problems, lawsuits, leasing defaults, unprofitable operations.

The Garrett Group used strategies that dealt with all of these problems head-on and saved many of these businesses. In fact, I had an eighty percent success rate. In comparison, small businesses that go into bankruptcy have a less than ten percent success rate.

During my consulting career, I worked with many troubled businesses in a variety of industries, both large and small. I would routinely see four to five potential new customers a week and had approximately ten active clients at any one time.

I restructured a $20 million travel business in severe financial trouble, developing and managing a debt-restructuring plan without the use of bankruptcy. This resulted in the company's debt being reduced from over $2.5 million to $300,000.

I stopped a bank foreclosure on a light maintenance company and negotiated a seven-year payback with the same bank at a substantially lower interest rate. After the restructuring, the same bank granted a line of credit to the company. I eliminated taxes and unsecured debt from the balance sheet totaling over $1 million, allowing the company to once again generate cash flow.

I also restructured a chemical distribution company that had several creditor judgments and pending executions against its assets.

In the end, I saved many businesses that would have otherwise failed. This kept companies in their respective communities and individuals employed.

Receiver Appointments

In addition to my consulting activities, in the early 1990s, I would routinely be appointed by the state of Wisconsin Circuit Court as a receiver under Chapter 128 of the Wisconsin statutes. This process was called the Assignment for the Benefit of Creditors. I was required to be bonded and responsible for liquidating a particular business and paying out the proceeds under a predetermined order of priority to creditors as was done under a federal bankruptcy proceeding. This state court-supervised process was much faster and less costly for creditors than a bankruptcy proceeding.

As an example, I liquidated a manufacturer of an industrial magnets company in Milwaukee, Wisconsin. In addition to selling its physical assets, such as accounts receivable, inventory, and machinery and equipment, I was able to negotiate the sale of its intangible assets—something that hardly ever happens in a bankruptcy proceeding. I sold the company's customer names, drawings, processes, and other intangibles to a competitor for $50,000 in cash. Creditors received substantially more from this state-court liquidation than they ever would have received if the owner had put his company through a Chapter 7 bankruptcy. As it turned out, this competitor also hired the owner of the business.

Another assignment involved the owner of a business that became delinquent on payroll taxes for $100,000. I was appointed by the circuit court to conduct the orderly liquidation of the property and pay the proceeds to its creditors.

Buying Troubled Companies

After having consulted with over two hundred financially troubled companies, I had the opportunity to purchase a consulting client's business, a structural component manufacturing company located in Appleton, Wisconsin. This company built wood trusses for the residential and agricultural construction industry. This particular company was being foreclosed on by its bank, had unpaid payroll tax obligations, and was threatened by several of its creditors with legal enforcement to pay. In fact, the company most likely had only a few months left to survive, which would have resulted in approximately thirty employees losing their jobs immediately. After striking an agreement with the existing owners, I met with the bank, purchased the assets directly from the bank, and started my new company, Truss Manufacturing, Inc., doing business under the trade name of Trussco. The result of this acquisition reduced over $900,000 in old company debt to less than $180,000, giving my new business a fresh start. Under my direction, Trussco continued to grow and remained profitable until I sold it to the general manager seven years later.

After the acquisition of Trussco, I decided to focus my attention on the acquisition of troubled companies. This was a hard decision since my consulting business was flourishing, but here was my opportunity to work in a business I had always thought would be more exciting. Over the next several years, I acquired over fifteen different troubled or underperforming companies in five different states in such industries as plastics, rubber, food, wood products, and industrial transformers. I even managed to be one of the founders of a start-up in the oil analytic and processing business, which was later sold to a private equity group. Most of these businesses I acquired were sold either to management or to competitors. Unfortunately, one of the companies in the wood-distribution business never worked out and had to be liquidated.

Acquisitions Portfolio

At the end of 2001, I had four businesses remaining, all managed day to day by a management team at their respective company locations. Since I was not an employee of any of these four companies, my expertise was provided to these managers through my management company, the Garrett Group, which was paid a management fee from these companies for my services. I went on site to each company routinely and spoke with all of the managers of these firms almost daily.

The first business, which I acquired in November 1997, was Western Rubber, Inc., a compression industrial rubber molder located in Indiana. Western had been a division of Western Consolidated Technology and was in the process of being liquidated by its owners when I completed the acquisition.

In June 1998, I purchased GAC Plastics, LLC, a high-tech plastic-injection molder located in upper Michigan that produced key plastic components for such customers as Ford, Chrysler, and Steelcase. The predecessor business had lost over $7 million over the preceding years and was in the process of slowly having its working capital drained since its bank was collecting its accounts receivable collateral and reducing its line of credit.

Then I purchased Badger Die Casting Corporation, an aluminum die-casting company located in Milwaukee, Wisconsin, in 1998. Before I acquired Badger, its annual sales had diminished to a point at which the company was no longer profitable. Badger turned out to be the source of my legal troubles. That story begins in the next chapter.

Finally, I acquired Ace Precision Castings, LLC in 2001. It was also in the aluminum die-casting business providing key components to companies such as CAT, John Deere, Kawasaki, Harley Davidson, and Paslode. Ace's predecessor was losing money and was forced by its bank to sell.

All together these four businesses had millions of dollars in sales and assets. Over four years from 1997 through 2001, these companies together produced over $107 million in sales and paid out over $44 million in employee wages, payroll taxes, and benefits. In addition, at the end of 2001, these companies had $20 million in collective company assets and employed almost four hundred individuals. In the face of these numbers, the government's prosecution of me was absurd.

Chapter 2

An Acquisition Gone Bad

A T THE END OF 2001, I still owned Badger Die Casting, the troubled business I had purchased in July 1998. I had bought Badger for a good reason. In 1997, after having purchased and successfully turned around a failing die-casting business in Minnesota and renaming it Northstar Die Casting, I wanted a second die-casting business to complement it. I hired a local business broker to conduct a search.

The broker found that Badger was for sale. After signing a confidentially agreement, I received an offering memorandum that described Badger's business in great detail, including a summary of its historical and expected financial data. According to the memorandum, Badger, originally established in 1919, was owned and operated by four members of the Strassman family.

The Strassmans' memorandum indicated that Badger's sales for the calendar years 1995 and 1996 had been $6.9 million and $6.8 million, respectively. Their EBIT (earnings before interest and taxes) for the same period was $688,000 and $619,000 respectively. Sales for 1997 were projected to be $6.8 million with the EBIT estimated at $670,000. They also projected sales and profits in 1998 and beyond to be $8.8 million with about $1.1 million in EBIT from their existing core customers.[1] Basically, the Strassmans were representing that Badger was a stable, strong, and healthy business with expanding sales well into the future.

To me, Badger seemed like an excellent fit with Northstar. Badger machined most of its die-casted parts, and there was a good possibility for it to cross-sell this service to Northstar's customers. Besides, there would be a reduction in costs for both companies with the consolidation of sales and administration functions into the Badger Milwaukee facility. However, I was concerned by the fact that Badger had a union and Northstar did not. I soon learned that Badger's union contract included a three percent increase in wages each year and an extremely expensive healthcare plan that covered substantially all employee healthcare claims. Badger paid eighty-five percent of the monthly health insurance premiums, while employees paid only fifteen percent. If I purchased Badger, I would be required to assume this union contract.

While this healthcare plan did provide excellent employee benefits, which would help in maintaining Badger's key employees and assist in recruiting new ones, I was apprehensive about the fact that the industry was changing and customers were demanding price reductions each year. I understood the implications of paying Badger's employees a three percent wage increase each year while at the same time having to give customers price decreases. Nevertheless, I proceeded with the acquisition because it appeared to be a stable business with good growth prospects.

After the Strassmans and their broker had received all their offers, they called me and gave me the good news: they had accepted my offer. Shortly thereafter, I brought in my local accounting firm and my lawyer to start the due-diligence process on Badger. The next milestone would be the completion of a thorough due diligence and then the drafting of the purchase agreement leading up the closing date.

During the next several weeks, which included several back-and-forth negotiations relating to purchase-agreement language, I noticed something unusual: monthly sales in January through April 1998 were not meeting the Strassmans' projections or their historical sales. I poured through the recent financial statements and came to the realization that these lower sales would substantially erode if not eliminate Badger's earnings. I knew a company without earnings was worth no more than the liquidation value of its assets.

Since the plan was to complete the purchase in just a few months, I was concerned not only about these recent sale declines but also about the likelihood that Badger's sales would continue to erode going forward. Did the Strassmans know something they were not disclosing? They would not be the first sellers to try to cover up problems when selling a business. In any event, I quickly concluded that this deal, at the price I had offered, was just too risky.

I called the broker and explained to her that due to Badger's recent sales dropoff, I would not be interested in completing the purchase at the current price. The broker and the Strassmans were obviously quite disappointed; however, they suggested that they would entertain a price concession. After having several meetings with the broker and the Strassmans, we agreed to a plan whereby John Strassman would meet with Badger's customers and assess their sales for the remaining year. I hoped this would provide sufficient information so that I could renegotiate the deal and end up with a price that was reasonable based on these lower sales numbers and earnings.

After meeting with several of Badger's key customers, John Strassman put together a projection of sales for 1998 totaling around $5.8 million. I knew that in the event he misrepresented these forecasts to bolster Badger's sales projection, I would have recourse against his $800,000 promissory note due in addition to suing him for damages.

Based on these revised sales numbers and lower anticipated profits, I submitted a letter to the broker, stating that I would purchase Badger if I received a $670,000 reduction in the purchase price. Shortly thereafter, I received word that they had agreed, but they stressed the point that we needed to close this deal quickly. Although I continued to be skeptical about Badger's true sales and profits, I knew that I had the protection of the Representation and Warranty section of the purchase agreement since the Strassmans explicitly agreed to be liable if they materially misrepresented information provided relating to Badger's business.

We finally closed the deal in July 1998. The final purchase price was approximately $5 million. The Strassmans received around $4.2 million in cash and a promissory note of $790,000.

I personally invested $100,000 and guaranteed $4 million, which I had borrowed from the LaSalle Bank as part of the purchase price, resulting in my family's entire net worth being put on the line with this deal. But I was excited about the prospects of increasing Badger's sales and profits and making it a better business.

Despite my hopes and my efforts, sales continued to deteriorate. It became quickly evident to me that 1998 sales would not end up as the Strassmans had predicted. With these lower sales, my evaluation indicated that Badger would start losing money and that something had to be done immediately. To stabilize the situation, I made the difficult decision to move key customers from Northstar to Badger, which meant the closing of Northstar. But I had to save Badger even if it meant sacrificing Northstar.

As it turned out, at the end of 1998, total sales at Badger ended up at $5.4 million, which was comprised of approximately $4.7 million from Badger's core sales from my purchase and approximately $680,000 in sales transferred down from Northstar. Still, Badger had posted a loss of about $150,000 for the year.[2] The realization set in that I had screwed up and overpaid for Badger. The Strassmans had again overstated their sales by perhaps embellishing the customers' projections.

I knew this difference in sales from the $5.8 million presented by the Strassmans and the actual sales for 1998 of $4.7 million—a difference of $1.1 million—would cost me approximately $500,000 each year in contribution margin, and I was not happy. I immediately contacted my attorney to see what could be done. Badger was a company slowly going out of business because of declining sales, and the Strassmans had cleverly sold it before it did. However, I also knew that the business of acquisitions is risky and you never know what you are buying until you are inside the company. I felt I was up for the challenge of saving this almost eighty-year-old company.

In the meantime, my attorney sent out a letter informing the Strassmans of their breach involving representations made in the purchase agreement, which included misrepresenting Badger's sales, a leaking roof, and nonpayment of a well-monitoring system that they had installed before the closing. In addition to outlining these damages, he indicated that payment on their promissory note would be withheld until this matter was resolved. The Strassmans sued me for payment on their promissory note, and I sued them for their many misrepresentations of Badger's business. We ended up settling for an approximately $190,000 reduction of their $790,000 promissory note, but, as it turned out, it was not nearly enough.

Rebuilding Badger

One of Badger's problems was that it had not updated its plant and equipment in many years. I had prepared a detailed business plan that included spending money on additional plant equipment to substantially improve productivity to allow Badger to double its sales to $10 million per year. This meant that Badger would need to borrow more money from LaSalle Bank to purchase more equipment and expand its labor force. I would be required to personally guarantee these additional loans.

Randy Lubben, the sales manager at Northstar in Minneapolis, moved down to Milwaukee to help with the transition of Northstar's customers to Badger. He also became Badger's vice president of sales and marketing responsible for Badger's sales development. This was quite a promotion for Lubben, as the job included a pay increase, leased car, and other company benefits. I had him sign a new employment and non-compete agreement before he started in March 1999.

I spent a considerable amount of time going through each of the line items of Badger's profit-and-loss statements looking for hidden opportunities to reduce expenses. Among many other profit-enhancing activities, I set up purchasing guidelines and budgets in all Badger departments to control costs and spending.

My efforts at Badger did start to pay off. In 1999, sales increased substantially, many new employees were added, and Badger became profitable. But I would soon be reminded just how challenging running a financially troubled business really is.

Chapter 3

The Challenge of Remaining Profitable

KEEPING BADGER PROFITABLE and cash-positive was an ongoing struggle. Even though my team grew sales to almost double from what they had been under the previous owners, the higher costs associated with getting these new sales out the door and to customers on time eroded profits.

Other events also put a severe strain on the business. As Badger's CEO and president, I made many critical decisions every year. But admittedly two of these decisions turned out to be disastrous and made a difficult situation even worse. These errors were (1) stepping down from running Badger day-to-day and installing a new president and (2) changing to a self-funded healthcare plan rather than reducing the level of benefits to reduce costs. Nevertheless, my team and I did the best we could to keep Badger together moving forward.

Operational Problems

The year 1999 ended up being a great one for Badger in terms of profitability. Sales had grown almost 100% to $9.8 million, and EBIT (earnings before interest and taxes) for the year were over $640,000.[3] However, this rapid increase in sales created other problems. Our past-due orders mounted, shipments were late, and customers were complaining. Lacking time to hire new employees, I implemented a Saturday shift at the plant to enable the company to catch up.

Since I was unable to spend the necessary time at Badger to adequately oversee its new challenges due to my other acquisition investments, I decided to hire a full-time senior manager as Badger's president. This manager could then focus full-time on making sure Badger's customers were satisfied and that Badger was profitable.

After several weeks of searching, on May 22, 2000, I hired and appointed Don Schlueter as Badger's new president and chief operating officer. I took the position of Badger's chief executive officer. Schlueter was to report directly to me. Mr. Schlueter's credentials showed him to be a seasoned manufacturing manager with successful extensive manufacturing experience over twenty-five years.

During the months of Schlueter's tenure, sales remained strong but profits remained weak since production expenses were excessive. I met each month with Schlueter to review in detail Badger's previous month's financials. He convinced me that he had the experience and skills necessary and would turn things around.

To my shock and dismay, when I received the December 2000 financials in the middle of January 2001, they showed that in December Badger had lost over $560,000 in just one month. As it turned out, Badger lost almost $800,000 for calendar year 2000. On January 21, 2001, I terminated Schlueter's employment with Badger and immediately took over the position of president responsible for day-to-day operations. At that point, I was unsure if these losses had damaged Badger's business beyond repair. I knew that the loss of almost $800,000 in such a short period of time could be a final blow to its business, but I was determined to return Badger to profitability once again.

Accelerating Healthcare Costs

Badger's union contract required that the company provide its employees with healthcare coverage. But according to the contract, Badger "reserves the right to select the insurance carrier or become self-insured, provided the benefits and administration are substantially equal to those in effect."[4] Up to that point, Badger had always provided its employees with a "fully funded" group healthcare plan, which meant that the insurance company pays for all healthcare claims directly after the employee's annual out-of-pocket deductibles.

Every year, Thresa Palkowski, Badger's human resources director, would get bids from insurance companies in order to find the best price while maintaining the same level of healthcare benefits for employees. Palkowski had held this position under the previous owners and continued in this capacity after I purchased Badger in 1998. Calendar year 2001 was no exception, and as the bids came in, we selected United Healthcare as our provider, to begin January 1, 2001.

The United plan was an excellent plan for the employees in that it covered most employee claims with little, if any, annual deductible for employees to pay. However, the cost was quite high for Badger: the monthly premium was approximately $42,000 for about one hundred employees, of which employees paid fifteen percent through payroll deductions. This resulted in an almost

$430,000 annual insurance cost to Badger. Furthermore, even though United provided a particular bid for monthly premiums, they had the right under the contract to increase premium rates upon specific notification.[5]

Indeed, within a few months, Badger received notice from United that its monthly premiums were to increase from approximately $42,000 a month to around $60,000. This meant Badger would be socked with an additional $184,000 per year, bringing Badger's annual cost toward the healthcare plan to $614,000 per year. This was an expense Badger clearly could not afford, especially after having lost almost $800,000 during the prior year.

I could have chosen to meet with the union and negotiate an increase in employee contributions or a reduction in healthcare benefits to keep the cost to Badger at a level it could afford. With the benefit of hindsight, I wish I had done that. But instead, I set out to investigate whether there was a way to provide Badger employees with the same level of benefits without an increase in cost.

Going Self-Insured

In the course of my research, I learned about a concept called "self-funded" healthcare. My insurance agent explained to me that Badger would hire a third-party administrator (TPA) to reconcile Badger's healthcare claims received from employee healthcare providers. As employee claims were submitted, the TPA would determine if the claims were covered under allowable treatments of the healthcare plan and if the employee deductible had been met. If the claims passed the test, the TPA would submit a request to Badger to fund payment. Badger would be responsible to pay all the claims above the employee's annual out-of-pocket deductible.

The idea was that Badger would function like an insurance company itself. It would collect monthly premium contributions from employees and set the deductible that each employee was responsible for each year. In theory, Badger would keep all the profit that would have gone to an outside insurance company, thereby lowering its overall healthcare costs. However, this plan seemed to me to be too risky because Badger would be responsible for all healthcare claims above each employee's deductible to the plan's lifetime maximum benefit per employee. If an employee got sick and needed $1 million worth of medical care, Badger would have to pay for it. That was of great concern to me.

So instead I found a second, more reasonable, option. Badger adopted a "partially self-funded" health insurance plan. Rather than taking all the risk above the employee deductible, Badger purchased what is called "stop-loss" insurance, which covered all healthcare claims above $30,000 per employee per year.

In their proposal, my insurance agent explained that a company called Medical Benefits Administrator (MBA) would be the TPA that would handle all Badger's healthcare claims. They also suggested that Badger use American National of Texas as the insurance company for the "stop-loss" coverage for claims in excess of $30,000 per year per employee. MBA had impressive credentials, which included being in business since 1982, and had paid out over $100 million in claims servicing over two hundred clients.

I thought I had found the best of both worlds in reducing Badger's healthcare costs while maintaining the same level of benefits for its employees. The difference between the United Healthcare existing annual premium of $504,000 ($42,000 a month) and the annual stop-loss healthcare premiums plus administration fees paid to MBA of approximately $95,000 per year would be used to fund employee healthcare claims, and Badger would keep the rest. In other words, the difference between these two numbers, $409,000, would be used to fund each employee's annual healthcare claims between their annual deductible and the $30,000. Our insurance agent looked at the historical claims and, although not a guarantee of future claims, determined that Badger could save money. Indeed, self-funded healthcare plans were widely used by other businesses in our state.

I instituted the MBA healthcare plan at Badger as well as at my other two businesses. I believed in this new plan so much that I enrolled my family in it. This one decision, although made with the best of intentions for my employees and Badger, would end up being the central issue in my criminal prosecution.

Badger was required by its union contract to inform employees of the change in healthcare plans before the effective date of July 1, 2001.[6] I instructed Thresa Palkowski to publish a notice in accordance with the contract. This was nothing unusual since she would routinely publish other union notices as required, and I had no concern that she would not handle this task properly. In fact, she handled almost all union interactions and generally interpreted union-contract language as part of her responsibility as Badger's human relations director. Palkowski posted the meeting notice regarding the insurance change on June 26, 2001. I received a copy in my mailbox at Badger but did not pay much attention to it.

MBA handled the sign-up sessions of Badger employees at the Badger plant on June 26, 2001. The plan was to have only two or three employees meet with MBA at a time so that Badger would not have to shut down its production with a company-wide meeting. During these meetings, Badger employees were told of the change in healthcare plan, who the administrator of the new MBA plan was, and if there were any changes from the old plan.[7] Badger employees also received temporary ID cards that day that clearly indicated that MBA was their new medical administrator.[8] I was not at the Badger plant that day but was told that the sign-up process went smoothly.

The MBA healthcare plan was similar to Badger's old plan through United Healthcare. Each Badger employee had to show an insurance card when visiting a doctor or the hospital. The healthcare provider would then submit this claim directly to MBA. MBA would then take these claims and check that these visits were indeed covered according to Badger's healthcare plan document, since Badger would not cover all medical services or treatments employees would receive. MBA would then fax these claims weekly to Badger for payment.

The first set of claims from MBA were shocking: over $50,000 worth for July. Badger had already paid MBA about $11,000 for the stop-loss insurance and administration for July 2001. I became very concerned. After checking into the claims, it appeared that July had been an exceptional month with higher-than-normal claims. But I still wondered how this new MBA plan was going to save Badger money when we had just paid out $62,000 for healthcare in July as compared to our old healthcare group premium costs of $42,000 a month.

But these higher than unanticipated healthcare expenses were just a start. Healthcare claims would continue to escalate well beyond Badger's ability to pay them as ever increasing tight cash flow continued to cause major problems as you will learn in the next chapter.

Chapter 4

Squeezed by the Bank

I HAD USED LaSALLE BANK as the lender to provide my financing needs for both the purchase of Badger and for ongoing loans such as a line of credit and capital equipment purchases. From the beginning I had maintained an excellent relationship with the bankers who initially managed my account.

Badger had loans with LaSalle Bank through its asset-based lending division. Most small businesses use either bank financing or an asset-based lender. Asset-based lenders in particular will lend varying percentages against different types of assets but generally lend only on hard assets and monitor the quality and level of these assets regularly. Back in 1998, a standard type asset-based lending agreement allows for eighty-five percent advance on eligible receivables, fifty percent on eligible inventory, and eighty percent on hard assets such as machinery, equipment, and real estate. This involves continuous reporting by the company and on-site audits by the asset-based lender. If a business is using this type of lending for working capital and wants to borrow money from its line of credit, then its managers will be required to fill out what's called a borrowing base certificate, or BBC. This BBC lists such things as accounts receivable balances and inventory levels. These asset levels will determine the amount of loans available to the company.

A different type of lender to businesses is a bank. Similarly, banks generally lend on the company's hard assets; however, their auditing, reporting, and paperwork to draw down on a line of credit is considerably less stringent than that of the asset-based lender. Both Badger and Western had asset-based lending loans from LaSalle National Bank.

Bank Management Change

As I said, I had always enjoyed an excellent relationship with LaSalle Bank in Chicago. Initially, LaSalle had financed the acquisition of Western Rubber in 1997, then the Badger deal, and then provided a line of credit and term loan with another one of my companies. LaSalle also provided Badger with additional financing along the way for capital equipment when needed through what was referred to as capx (capital expenditure) term loans. The bankers at LaSalle were friendly and appeared to take a real interest in the success of my businesses. However, things suddenly changed considerably.

One day, I received a call from my banker at LaSalle, who informed me that he and his two bosses would be leaving LaSalle's asset-based lending division and a new team would be taking over. At the time, he was handling separate lending facilities at three of my companies, which were comprised of several loans totaling several millions of dollars. Right off the bat, I was very concerned. I knew that this man strongly supported my businesses within the bank, and this change was not going to be a good thing. I prepared for the worst.

A few weeks later, I met with the new asset-based senior manager, Richard Simons, and two of his subordinates, John Littrell and Matt Sessa at Badger. During their introduction, Simons indicated that he and Littrell had come from the asset-based division of CIT Group. Simons explained to me that Sessa would be Badger's day-to-day contact. I knew CIT Group by reputation, not a very good one. The CIT workout bankers were cutthroat and would generally take action first and then ask questions later.

After several weeks had passed and these new bankers had settled in at LaSalle, I made some phone calls and finally figured out what had happened. Due to the slowdown in business in late 1999, early 2000, especially in the manufacturing sector, LaSalle had been experiencing major problems with their asset-based loan portfolio, and these new bankers were obviously brought in to "kick some ass and clean things up."

We had always made our loan payments on time, but Badger and Western did not always meet the stringent performance covenants in the LaSalle loan agreements. The bank had always waived these minor infractions each year.

After taking back control of Badger with Don Schlueter's departure as Badger's president and chief operations officer, I began to see some good signs. After a small loss of approximately $18,000 on sales of around $800,000 for the month of January 2001, Badger started to become profitable once again. February through October 2001 were all profitable months, and the year ended with a profit of a little over $254,000. Nevertheless, the loss of almost $800,000 in 2000 caused Badger major cash-flow problems. My new bankers at LaSalle had lost interest early on and informed me that it was time for Badger to find a new bank. They would not be renewing Badger's line of credit.

Finding a new lender would not be an easy task. Due to the economy, banks and other asset-based lenders had largely reduced their lending, especially to manufacturing companies. Asset values such as manufacturing machinery, equipment, and industrial real estate values had declined considerably, reducing the amount a business could borrow using these assets as collateral. Faced with these industry-wide obstacles, Badger had its own specific problems that further diminished its chances of finding a new loan. Although Badger was again profitable in 2001, it had lost almost $800,000 in 2000, which I knew would create doubt with a new lender. I prepared a detailed loan package and presented it to over ten banks and asset-based lenders, but I was unable to secure a new loan. I now had to seriously consider selling Badger as a way to resolve the bank problem.

Cash-Flow Squeeze

Over the months, as I was attempting to find a new lender for Badger, my relationship with LaSalle Bank's new management became even more tenuous. LaSalle assigned a banker responsible for approving Badger's day-to-day loan advances from our line of credit who worked almost exclusively with our controller, Ron Bussan. Bussan was responsible for determining Badger's daily cash needs and completing a borrowing base certificate (BBC) that he forwarded to the bank. Money was then deposited in Badger's account by LaSalle Bank that same day. The line-of-credit loan agreement allowed Badger to borrow an amount up to eighty-five percent of its accounts receivables and fifty percent of its inventory.

As time went on, LaSalle Bank routinely reduced Badger's loan availability on its line of credit by eliminating certain customer accounts receivables and inventory that it exclusively deemed inadequate to use for lending on collateral that had been acceptable under the old LaSalle Bank management. This tactic is nothing new in the asset-based lending industry. Asset-based lenders use this approach to squeeze a company's cash flow, thus pressuring it to find alternative sources of capital or abruptly face going out of business.

Although I had already invested $100,000 when I purchased Badger and was on the hook personally for the repayment of several millions of dollars of loans made to Badger from LaSalle Bank, I was now faced with having to risk even more capital to keep Badger afloat. Nevertheless, at that point, I was not willing to let Badger go down.

I provided Badger with a short-term loan for $400,000 to be paid back as soon as possible with nominal interest. As it turned out, during the early part of 2001, Badger did manage to pay back some of this loan. However, over $230,000 plus interest was never repaid.

Badger's cash-flow problems continued. In June 2001, Badger's controller, Ron Bussan, informed me that Badger had inadequate loan availability on its line of credit at LaSalle Bank to meet the next week's payroll totaling $65,000. LaSalle was unwilling to help. Again, I was faced with the choice of putting more money into Badger or closing up shop and liquidating the business. I had not even been paid back for the last loan I had provided Badger. My personal cash was tight, and the only available funds I could get on such short notice were from my family's line of credit secured by a second mortgage on my house in Franklin, Wisconsin.

On June 20, 2001, I wired $65,000 to Badger's bank account to meet that week's payroll. This loan never ended up being repaid, and I was stuck personally paying off my second mortgage on our home.

The more time that went by, the more apparent it became that buying Badger had been a very bad decision. When Badger needed cash, either due to the bank's continuous squeezing in its effort to force me to find alternative financing or Badger having a short-term cash crunch, I was the one who had to step up to the plate and provide the cash. In addition to the multimillion dollar personal guarantee I had already provided on Badger's bank debt, I was now having to put my home on the line. I also reduced my compensation to a couple of thousand dollars a month but still devoted my full-time effort to Badger. As time went on, LaSalle Bank monitored all of Badger's cash disbursements and restricted our payment of the employee healthcare claims that had been accumulating.

At that point, I could have easily just thrown in the towel and given the keys to the bank or just filed bankruptcy, but I knew Badger would not survive that. I am not a quitter—never have been. I was responsible for the legacy of an eighty-year-old company and over one hundred employees and their families who desperately depended on their jobs. I was an experienced and trained senior manager who had saved numerous financially distressed companies, and I was determined to keep Badger in business. If I could not find an appropriate replacement for LaSalle, I would find a suitable new owner who would continue to grow Badger well into the future.

Chapter 5

A Time to Sell

LaSalle Bank was breathing down my neck to take them out of their loans; I had provided Badger with personal loans and was not getting repaid; I had provided Badger with almost $4 million in personal guarantees securing their loans; and I was working on Badger's business nearly full time and not getting adequately compensated. I finally made the decision to sell Badger.

I looked around the Midwest at several different business brokers, merger & acquisition brokers, and investment bankers who I thought would be successful in locating a new owner for Badger. Investment bankers did deals similar to the ones handled by merger & acquisition brokers but generally larger. I focused my attention on a small investment-banking firm located in Chicago called Resource Financial Corporation (RFC).

In September 2001, I met with the principals of RFC at Badger. After their evaluation of Badger's financial statements and general information, they concluded that Badger could be sold for approximately $7 million, possibly more. This would be a gross sale price, which would require that I deliver Badger free and clear of all bank and other secured debt. This price made sense to me since it was based on a market multiple of Badger's previous twelve-month earnings before interest, taxes, and depreciation (EBITDA). Badger's problem was not its EBITDA but rather its high interest expense: its balance sheet was layered with debt and insufficient to fund the operations of Badger.

An Employee's Interest

In the meantime, Randy Lubben, Badger's vice president of sales and marketing, expressed to me an interest in purchasing Badger. Although I considered him a good candidate since he knew the industry well, I was concerned about his ability to complete such a transaction since he did not have any experience in operating an entire company or acquiring a business. I also questioned him about his financial capability to purchase Badger. Lubben said he had $200,000 available from his father-in-law in addition to some personal funds for a down payment. At the conclusion of our conversation, I told him that I would consider his interest but needed him to sign a confidentiality agreement before he could proceed with his review. He did sign this agreement, and in doing so agreed to keep all information provided to him confidential and to use it only for the purpose of evaluating his potential purchase of Badger's business.[9]

At the time, I really had no concern that Lubben would do anything other than use this confidential information legally. Besides, Lubben's employment and non-compete agreement, in which he had agreed to use "his best efforts to further enhance and develop Badger's internal organization, operations, business affairs, interest and welfare," was still in effect.[10]

During the following weeks, I provided Lubben with detailed financial information on Badger's expenses and projections—information to which he did not have access in the regular course of his job. For example, I provided Lubben with Badger's historical financial statement data, projections on future balance sheets and profit-and-loss statements, and the contact names and phone numbers of Badger's bankers at LaSalle Bank. I told Lubben that he was free to contact these bankers during his evaluation process.

I met with Lubben several times to answer his questions and provided him with additional information. During one of our meetings, I explained to him my terms and conditions of a sale, including that the buyer would pay off the balance of the LaSalle bank debt; assume the equipment lease Badger had with my company Franklin Leasing; and assume responsibility for employees' outstanding benefits such as vacation payments, accrued 401(k) liability, healthcare claims, and employees accrued payroll. I told Lubben that I would not be looking for the buyer to repay my loans but would require a non-compete agreement—of $300,000 to be paid over sixty months—that would restrict me from conducting business with Badger's customers.

After several weeks of negotiations and allowing him access to Badger's confidential information, Lubben told me that he would agree to some of my terms but would not agree to assume responsibility for Badger's employee benefits, healthcare claims, or the $300,000 non-compete agreement. This was a deal-breaker for me, so I told him that I was not interested in his offer and would pursue other interested buyers. I assured him that I believed his position with a new buyer would be certain due to his experience and relationships with all Badger's customers.

Other Interested Buyers

RFC brought in several buyer candidates. Early in the process, I received a reasonable offer from a competing die-caster in Missouri. However, it was based on closing the Badger plant and moving all of its customers to the buyer's plant in Missouri. Milwaukee would lose a long-standing employer and all my workers would lose their jobs. I wanted Badger to remain in Milwaukee and keep its workers employed. As this proposal was not what I was looking for, I declined the offer.

I met with several other potential buyers, but one particular party appeared to be the best candidate. A private equity firm called Capital for Business (CFB) and two former managers who had previously owned a successful die-caster, which they eventually sold, had teamed up looking for a die-casting acquisition. CFP made an offer in the $3.5 million range, well below what RFC had indicated, but I knew it would be adequate to take out LaSalle Bank and cover any remaining employee benefits due. Time was running out, and I had to get a deal done quickly since LaSalle continued to exert pressure and was becoming even more impatient with each passing day. I called my contact at RFC and asked him to arrange the details of the sale and wrap things up.

The deal structure, which was outlined, involved CFB purchasing Badger's assets directly from LaSalle Bank for the balance of the bank's loans. The deal also included payment of all outstanding employee benefits and employee healthcare claims by CFP per my requirement. I realized that I would not be getting my personal loans repaid or any compensation from the sale; however, I would be receiving $300,000 to be paid over sixty months in exchange for my personal agreement not to compete with Badger's customers. The equipment Badger was using was owned by my company, Franklin Leasing, and would continue to be leased by CFB's new company.

Since time was of the essence, we discussed moving toward a quick closing in just a few weeks after some additional due-diligence work by CFB. I was confident that we would conclude a sale to CFB.

Little did I know that the bankers at LaSalle and one of my key employees at Badger were planning something different.

Chapter 6

An Insider Takeover

ON TUESDAY, APRIL 16, 2002, I started the day as I would have any other weekday by working in my home office. After completing some paperwork, I called Badger just after lunch to check my messages. Badger had an automated phone system, which answered "Badger Die Casting" before the caller had the opportunity to select a department. However, when I called in this time, to my surprise the recording said, "Wisconsin Die Casting." I was baffled.

I immediately called my attorney, Harold Laufer. He said he would check into the matter and get back to me. When he called back, he told me that that morning Randy Lubben's newly created business, Wisconsin Die Casting, had purchased all of Badger's assets from LaSalle Bank. I asked him what could be done about this, and he suggested I meet with bankruptcy counsel at his firm. I knew tipping Badger into bankruptcy to challenge the sale between LaSalle and Lubben would be extremely expensive and might even risk Badger's ability to continue as a going concern, so I ruled out that option. I thought there was no way that either Lubben or LaSalle Bank would get away with this.

Later that day, I contacted RFC to let them know what had happened at Badger. They were obviously very upset since they had spent many weeks working on this project and planned on completing the sale to CFP and collecting their commission. They were initially angry with me and accused me of not letting them know the extent of Badger's problems with LaSalle Bank. However, I explained to them that they knew LaSalle wanted out of the Badger loans and that the planning and negotiations between Lubben and LaSalle had been deliberately hidden from me and there really wasn't much I could have done to stop this from taking place.

So, the question that begs for an answer is how could Lubben have acquired Badger without my knowledge, consent, or approval? I was the sole owner of all Badger's voting stock. Well, the answer is rather shocking.

As I mentioned earlier, before providing Lubben with any confidential information, I'd had him sign a confidentiality agreement whereby he agreed to use the private financial information only for the purpose of pursuing his interest in acquiring Badger. At the time, I was also aware that Lubben had signed an employment and non-compete agreement several years earlier whereby he agreed to promote Badger's business, not cause it harm, and to not compete against it. At that time, I had absolutely no concerns that Lubben would do anything to harm Badger, its business, or my interest in Badger.

However, I later found out through examination of documents recovered in the LaSalle Bank litigation that I could not have been more wrong about Lubben's intentions. As it turned out, shortly after I turned down Lubben's offer to purchase Badger, Lubben proceeded to hire an attorney and started negotiating directly with LaSalle Bank without my knowledge. This led to several phone conversations, emails, and document drafts between Lubben, his attorney, and LaSalle Bank. Lubben then set up his new company, Wisconsin Die Casting, LLC, during the first few days of April 2002. The final agreement between LaSalle Bank and Lubben was signed the morning of April 16, 2002 when his new company acquired Badger's assets. Lubben immediately proceeded to march down to Badger and announced to all of Badger's employees that he was the new owner of Badger's assets and business.

So how could LaSalle Bank sell Badger's assets without my consent or approval? Actually, it's pretty easy. Under state uniform commercial code (UCC), LaSalle just needed one technical violation of the loan agreement and to deliver a letter to Badger and other secured creditors of this default and LaSalle's intent to foreclose. Once these two conditions were met, they could take back all their collateral (other than real estate) without filing a lawsuit or otherwise requiring any court supervision. In my case, although I was making all of Badger's loan payments each month on time, Badger was "technically" in violation of performance covenants in their loan agreement. In fact, these were minor violations that had been routinely waived in prior years by LaSalle Bank. However, now they were sufficient to permit LaSalle to foreclose if they chose to do so, which they did. I had received this foreclosure letter from LaSalle but didn't think anything of it since it was consistent with the plan I had discussed with LaSalle Bank to sell Badger's assets to CFB.

Next, if LaSalle intended to sell Badger's assets to someone else, they needed to establish the value of these assets. LaSalle previously had had a liquidation "forced sale" appraisal completed on Badger's equipment. The bank had hired someone to value the inventory in a forced-sale scenario. After adding the forced-sale value of the equipment together with the reduced inventory and accounts receivable, they came up with a total-asset-value dollar amount. Magically, but not surprisingly, Badger's assets came out to be less than Badger's loan balance due LaSalle Bank of approximately $3.2 million. Therefore, the way the transaction worked was that Lubben purchased all Badger's assets for the assumption of Badger's debt owed to LaSalle Bank.

I am sure that behind the scenes Lubben was able to convince LaSalle Bank that he was the better buyer because he had relationships with all Badger's customers and could complete a transaction much faster than CBP. Lubben pulled this off—all while working at Badger as an employee and collecting his salary—without my knowledge. His conduct violated his employment agreement, his non-compete agreement, and the confidentially agreement he signed promising to use the information he received about Badger for the sole purpose of acquiring Badger business and assets from Badger Die Casting. I trusted him as one of my key senior Badger employees. But business is full of lessons, and this one lesson I learned the hard way: Don't be so trusting!

The day of Lubben and LaSalle Bank's takeover of Badger's business and assets was also the last day Badger was open for business, as all its cash and assets were removed by LaSalle Bank leaving it no resources with which to operate. In fact, during that morning, while Badger was still operating—just as it had for the previous eighty years—Lubben walked in and announced that he had just purchased all of Badger's assets and that Badger was no more. Lubben then called a group meeting and told all Badger employees that they would have to interview with his new company if they were to be employed going forward. No one was ever fired from Badger. Lubben just came in and took over.

In fact, Lubben's takeover was quite simple. He set up a new company, Wisconsin Die Casting, purchased all Badger's assets from LaSalle Bank, then walked into Badger and took over the operations, including Badger's customers, and reemployed the workers at his new company. This left Badger without assets, customers, or going concern value, but all its remaining debt. It was apparent to me that Lubben and the bank's plan was to take all of Badger's assets and leave behind all the employee benefits for me to deal with.

Chapter 7

The Start of Litigation

DESPITE THE FACT THAT LUBBEN had taken over all Badger's assets and left all the liability behind, the union was hell-bent on making sure I paid their employee benefits. The union claimed that Badger and I owed their member employees all outstanding unpaid health claims, union dues, and some 401(k) contributions. In fact, later on I would come to find out that Lubben's new company was legally responsible, as a matter of federal law, for all Badger's employee benefits since he was aware of these liabilities before he took over Badger's assets. This was beside the fact that I had demanded that he pay these employee benefits before he took over Badger.

NLRB Complaint

The United Electrical, Radio, and Machine Workers Union—Local 1112, which had represented Badger employees, started their legal process against me by filing a complaint with the National Labor Relations Board (NLRB). The NLRB is an *independent agency of the U.S. government* charged with investigating and remedying *unfair labor practices*.[11] This is quite a convenient government agency for unions since they can simply file a complaint against an employer, and the NLRB will do all the heavy lifting in adjudicating their complaint without cost to the union.

Just a few weeks after Badger was taken over by Lubben, the Badger union filed with the NLRB an unfair labor practices complaint against Badger Die Casting along with other companies of mine that had nothing to do with Badger Die Casting or the union. The union alleged, among other things that Badger:

> failed and refused to bargain in good faith by unilaterally altering its health insurance coverage without giving notice to the union and an opportunity to bargain. The union did not learn about the employer's actions until late November 2001;

> failed and refused to bargain in good faith by failing to adequately fund its health insurance plan and by failing to pay employees healthcare bills despite repeated assurances that it would make such payment;

> and failed and refused to bargain in good faith by failing to make required payments to its 401(k).

Although, I was aware that Badger had unpaid healthcare claims in the approximate amount of $325,000 at the time it was forced to close, I was unaware that approximately $20,000 in 401(k) contributions were past due. This was because Badger's payroll and payroll-related items were handled by its controller, Ron Bussan, and his staff. Bussan, like the other former Badger employees, was now working for Lubben's new company, Wisconsin Die Casting.

The union also claimed that Badger had altered its insurance coverage without giving notice or providing the union with the opportunity to bargain. That claim by the union was patently false. As I explained earlier, Badger's human relations director, Thresa Palkowski, had provided the union with proper notice of the change in healthcare coverage from United Healthcare to Medical Benefits Associates (MBA) at the time that the change had been made. Also, before they signed up, union employees were provided with an explanation as to the new healthcare plan and how it worked. They were allowed to ask any questions about this plan. It was MBA personnel, not me or any other Badger employee, who conducted the sign-up sessions with union employees in June 2001. They handed out brochures and temporary insurance cards that clearly presented who MBA was and how the new healthcare plan worked before the plan started.

If the union and its employees later decided that they did not like the self-funded health insurance that Badger had selected, then they should not have agreed to that provision as spelled out in the union contract, which explicitly allowed Badger management to select a self-funded health insurance plan. Union contract language clearly stated that Badger "reserves the right to select the insurance carrier or become self-insured."[12] Filing these frivolous NLRB charges and misrepresenting the facts was a clear misuse of this government agency and a waste of taxpayer money. But unfortunately, unions use the NLRB this way all the time. Unions love to bargain and use their leverage whenever possible, even if, as in this case, they had agreed to certain provisions in a union contract.

So why didn't the union go after Lubben and his new company? It's simple. WDC was now their employer. They were all in the middle of negotiating a new contract, which meant the continuation of union dues paid to the union. The union was certainly not going to do anything to bite the hand that fed it. Besides, it had me in its cross-hairs.

After receiving notice of these charges from the NLRB, I hired attorneys Bob Bartel and Mark Johnson with the law firm of Krukowski & Costello to represent me. Bartel and I met with the NLRB and provided them with a lengthy affidavit regarding the union's allegations. As it turned out, the NLRB withdrew its complaint against me and all of my companies without a settlement.[13]

Union's Lawsuit

On July 11, 2002, the Badger union filed its own federal lawsuit against, among others, Badger Die Casting, Garrett Group, Wisconsin Die Casting, and me personally. I hired attorney Robert Chapman out of Chicago who was recommended to me as a good civil litigator.

I believe the union filed its lawsuit because it received word that the NLRB was going to dismiss the complaint against me that the union had filed. Why else would the union spend thousands of dollars of its own money in legal fees attempting to win rather than let the NLRB spend taxpayer money instead?

In this lawsuit, they claimed that I and my other businesses were liable to the union and its members for unpaid healthcare benefits and 401(k) contributions. These were the same allegations made in the NLRB complaint against my companies and me. The union also sued Lubben's new company, but I heard through the grapevine that after Lubben signed a new union contract, they released his company from the lawsuit.

After several months of court hearings and legal documents filings, and after the union and I spent perhaps well over $200,000 in legal fees even before the trial started, I agreed to settle the case by paying approximately $150,000 to the union to be used for payment of union employee healthcare claims which they alleged totaled $400,000. Basically, what the union did in determining this settlement amount, which I agreed with, was to add up the amount already paid by employees in claims plus an amount they thought would settle the remaining claims with providers. As a result, the union agreed to dismiss the lawsuit against me and my companies with prejudice.[14]

Bank's Lawsuit

Meanwhile, the previous year, I had also sold Western Rubber. LaSalle Bank had been Western's lender as well and had preferred that I sell the company and pay off its loans. In fact, they were not interested in lending any more money to Western either. My first choice was to find a buyer who would keep Western at its current location in Goshen, Indiana. However, after contacting many potential buyers, we could find no one interested. I had assumed that it would be difficult since Western's physical plant was large and expensive to maintain and its equipment was old and outdated. As it turned out, the only reasonable offer we received was from Viking Polymer Solutions, LLC.

Viking agreed to purchase Western's key customers, their related accounts receivables, inventory, and the equipment needed to produce these customer parts. The remaining assets of Western would be my responsibility to sell. The sale of Western was finalized in February 2002 and the plant was closed at the end of that month. All proceeds of the sale went directly to LaSalle

Bank toward Western's loan balance. All that was left to do was liquidate Western's remaining assets.

I hired Western's general manager and Western's controller to handle that task. All of these funds went directly to LaSalle to continue to pay down their loan. In fact, since LaSalle had a first lien on all of Western's assets, using this money for any other purpose would have been illegal. After all this remaining equipment, receivables, and inventory were sold and collected and paid to LaSalle, there still remained an unpaid balance due LaSalle of around $550,000 which I had personally guaranteed.

In May 2002, just as I was getting ready to close on the sale of Badger to CFB, I put Western's real estate on the market for sale and assumed that it would be more than sufficient to pay off the Western loan balance. This was due to the fact that earlier LaSalle Bank had ordered a third-party appraisal that represented the value of Western's building to be in excess of $750,000, which LaSalle's own internal real estate department verified. However, the real estate never did sell.

As a result, LaSalle National Bank filed a lawsuit against my management company, Garrett Group, the company that held the real estate Western occupied; WRA Holdings; and myself based on my personal guarantee on Western Rubber loans. Although all Western's assets, except the real estate, had been sold and proceeds paid toward the loan balance, LaSalle apparently felt it necessary to sue me personally.

Suing the Bank

After LaSalle Bank sued my companies for the Western Rubber loan balance, I proceeded to mount a counterattack against the bank. In April 2003, my attorney filed an affirmative defense against LaSalle Bank claiming that my personal guarantees were not enforceable since LaSalle had provided me with an appraisal and an assessment stating that the value of Western's real estate was in excess of Western Rubber's loan balance and that I relied on their valuation before providing my personal guarantee of Western loans.

On the same day, I filed a counterclaim against LaSalle Bank claiming the bank had engaged in secret negotiations and conspired with Randy Lubben to take over Badger Die Casting and that LaSalle Bank had knowingly participated in providing substantial assistance in facilitating Lubben's breach of contract of his employment and non-compete agreements with Badger, causing Badger and myself substantial damage.

On August 28, 2006, after four years of litigation and having personally spent thousands of dollars in legal fees, LaSalle Bank and I reached an out-of-court settlement.

Chapter 8

Indicted

I T WAS CLEARLY THE UNION'S INTENT to do whatever it took to force me to pay Badger's unpaid healthcare and other benefits come hell or high water. The union had already filed a complaint with the NLRB and a lawsuit against me in federal court. Now they asserted what pressure they could in a new direction—by complaining to the Department of Labor (DOL). There were now two government agencies and the union's lawsuit all trying to get me to pay Badger employees' healthcare claims.

Although I felt bad that the Badger employees had gotten caught in the middle of this dispute, I was determined to legally compel LaSalle Bank and Randy Lubben to make good on all the employee benefits due even though the union and other government agencies were aggressively attacking me.

Criminal Investigation

The Department of Labor started its investigations based on allegations made by the Badger union president. Ron Bussan, Badger's controller, was now working for Lubben and was meeting with the DOL and other government agencies including the

FBI. Looking back, I am sure that Bussan and Lubben were doing everything they could to implicate me so as to take the spotlight off of their own conduct. Bussan had administered Badger's payroll and 401(k) plan and did not submit all employees 401(k) contributions to the plan administrator, and Lubben while employed at Badger, was misusing the financial information to which I gave him access.

One day during the summer of 2002, I received a call from Western's general manager who was handling Western's asset sale at the Western plant. He said he had received a federal subpoena from the U.S. Attorney's Office in Milwaukee requesting certain Western records, and he asked me what he should do. At first, I was surprised and had no clue why they would need anything from Western. We had been winding up the affairs at Western, and I had no idea why they would have any interest in any of Western's documents. In any event, I told him he needed to honor the subpoena and to provide the government with whatever they were looking for. I asked him to send me a copy of the subpoena.

Since the subpoena had come directly from the U.S. Attorney's Office and was titled "Subpoena in a Criminal Case," it was apparent that the DOL Investigator had convinced the U.S. Attorney's Office to pursue a criminal case against me. As I later learned, when a DOL investigator wants to bring a criminal case against someone, it has to persuade the local U.S. Attorney's Office to investigate and then prosecute the case. The DOL has no ability to bring a criminal case on its own.

Nevertheless, even though I could not figure out why the government would be investigating a criminal case against me, I now knew the Big Boys were involved and I did not want to take any chances that anything could spiral out of control. I had to find some expert help right away.

Heading off Problems

I reasoned that it would probably be best to hire a local attorney to make contact with the U.S. Attorney's Office to resolve any issues or misunderstanding. At the time, I had no evidence that anybody had done anything wrong let alone criminal, but I just thought it would be better to be safe than sorry.

After looking around and making some calls, I finally contacted attorney Stephen Glynn, who had been written up in local magazines and newspapers over the years as the best criminal attorney in southeastern Wisconsin. He appeared to have substantial experience representing white-collar criminal defendants in complex cases. In fact, I found a survey in one local magazine indicating that Glynn was the lawyer's lawyer when it came to criminal investigations—most, if not all, local attorneys would call Glynn if they had a criminal problem. I thought at the time that even though I did not think I had a criminal problem, he would likely have a very good relationship with the U.S. Attorney's Office.

I spoke with Glynn, who told me his initial charge would be $5,000 and that he would send a retainer agreement out immediately. The $5,000 retainer would be billed against his time and he would expect that I would replenish this amount in the event it ran out. He also said that if the case was resolved before the $5,000 retainer was exhausted, the full retainer would be considered earned. He further stated in his retainer agreement that "resolution of the case that quickly would reflect the advantage gained by this firm's quick response to your inquiry (which required setting aside other matters temporarily and unexpectedly), prompt work on your behalf, good reputation, and ability to react quickly and effectively because of prior experience with similar allegations. This is why we consider such a minimum earned fee to be fair and reasonable."

Glynn assured me he would contact the government about my situation, and I felt confident he would resolve any misunderstandings and resolve the matter quickly. I signed the agreement and sent the check.

"Nothing to Worry About"

Between July 2002 and November 2003, a period of almost a year and a half, I called Glynn several times to inquire about the status of the government's investigation. Each time we spoke, he told me that I had "nothing to worry about." What Glynn was telling me at the time made perfect sense. I knew I had done nothing wrong, certainly nothing criminal, and he made it sound as though he felt sure the government would complete its investigation and close the case. I went on with my life thinking everything would turn out fine.

Then, out of the blue, sometime in late November 2003, Glynn called me and told me that "things were heating up" at the U.S. Attorney's Office and that there was a good chance I would be indicted by a grand jury before year end.

All I could say was, "You've got to be kidding me! I thought you told me that I had nothing to worry about."

He responded that he would try to set up a meeting with the government before they brought my case before the grand jury so that we could sit down and discuss the matter and present our side of the story.

Glynn later called me to let me know that he had set up a meeting at the U.S. Attorney's Office in Milwaukee in mid-December. He suggested that I meet him at his office ten minutes prior so that we could walk over together. His office was right next door to the federal courthouse. I found it strange that he did not want to meet with me to discuss our presentation to the government and go over with me what things I should say or not say.

Government Meeting

Present at the meeting were two Department of Labor investigators, one named Jeffery Archbold, FBI Agent Terry Sparacino, and the prosecutor Assistant United States Attorney Gordon P. Giampietro.

After some small talk, Glynn told me to go ahead and tell my story. I proceeded to talk about my business of purchasing and revitalizing troubled companies. After about sixty seconds, I was abruptly, and I must say rudely, interrupted by Sparacino who said, "You're losing me." I had no idea why he would say that. He then slid over to me a single piece of Badger stationery containing the headline "Meeting Notice" and told me to read it. The language of the document stated that Badger was changing from United Healthcare to MBA effective July 1, 2001. Thresa Palkowski's name was typed on the bottom of this notice with the words "Posted 6/21/01." Palkowski as I mentioned earlier, was Badger's director of human resources who had been in charge of making sure employees knew about the change in healthcare plans.

The FBI agent said, "You told Thersa Palkowski to write that MBA was Badger's new health insurance carrier when in fact you knew that MBA was not an insurance carrier." I said, "You've got to be kidding me. I never told Thresa Palkowski that." He told me that Palkowski would testify that I had. I quickly realized that this meeting had nothing to do with telling my story or answering questions. Glynn and I left shortly thereafter.

While driving home, I was coming to the realization that this was becoming a very serious matter. On December 29, 2003, I sent Glynn a letter as follows:

> I am disappointed with the meeting we had at the U.S. Attorney's office. The other side clearly did not come to this meeting with an open mind interested in hearing my side of the story. The U.S. Attorney and their investigators apparently do not have all the relevant facts of this case, certainly not the financial records that tell the whole story. They are obviously influenced by the union's unsubstantiated allegations.
>
> I have always put my company and its employees and their needs at the top of my priority list. I have been wrongly accused and I have done nothing wrong and definitely have not committed any crimes as they have suggested.

In closing the letter I added:

> I am willing to provide any and all documents and information necessary to clear up this matter. After your review, I would like your thoughts on how we can proceed with a plan to resolve this matter quickly before I am possibly indicted."

Glynn never responded to my letter. But a few weeks later, he called to tell me that the government prosecutor told him they were taking my case to the grand jury and I was going to be indicted shortly.

My Indictment

In late January 2004, Glynn called to inform me that I had been indicted on January 21, 2004, on thirteen counts by a federal grand jury in the Southeastern District of Wisconsin. The indictment charged that I had violated certain federal criminal laws involving my ownership of Badger Die Casting and Western Rubber. Essentially, the indictment was broken into three parts.

First, it alleged that I had "converted" (a fancy legal term for stolen), with criminal intent, $52,126 of Badger and Western's employee payroll deductions intended to be used for their healthcare plans in violation of 18 U.S.C. §§ 664, 669 (counts 1 through 4).

Second, it alleged that I had converted, with criminal intent, $20,752 of Badger employee payroll deductions intended to be paid into their 401(k) plan in violation of 18 U.S.C. §664 (counts 5 through 9).

And finally, it claimed that I had made, with criminal intent, several false statements related to the Badger and Western healthcare plans in violation of 18 U.S.C. §1035 (counts 10 through 13).

After reading the indictment, I was puzzled. I had assumed this whole case was about the $400,000 in unpaid healthcare claims for Badger employees. Instead, I was charged with incidental amounts relating to Badger and Western that routinely were handled civilly by the Department of Labor. But as I eventually found out, my indictment was only one part of a master plan orchestrated by the prosecutor and union in their attempt to force me to pay the Badger healthcare claims.

Chapter 9

More Legal Actions

THE LITIGATION WAS MOUNTING. I now had a complaint filed against me by the NLRB; federal lawsuit filed against me by the union; and a criminal indictment filed against me by our federal government—all instigated by the union. At this point, I had spent well over $300,000 in legal fees related to business for which my average annual compensation was only around $110,000 per year as Badger's CEO and president. But little did I know that this was just the start of my problems surrounding Badger. I would be facing many more civil lawsuits and a brutal criminal prosecution which would push me and my family to the brink of our emotional capacity and extract over a million dollars more out of our personal savings in legal fees and settlements.

Suing Lubben

In April 2004, I filed a lawsuit against Lubben and his company, Wisconsin Die Casting, as a countercomplaint in the *LaSalle Bank v. Whiting* lawsuit. Initially, Lubben and his attorneys attempted to have my lawsuit dismissed based on their allegation that I didn't have the legal right to sue him in an Illinois state court. Nonetheless, after several months of depositions and other evidence discovery, my attorney filed a brief laying out the facts, including citations, that demonstrated exactly what had transpired regarding Lubben's secret takeover of Badger."[15]

The Court eventually ruled on Lubben's motion to dismiss the lawsuit on the issue of whether or not I had the legal right to sue Lubben in Illinois by finding that "evidentiary documents and depositions sufficiently support [Whiting's] claim that Lubben and WDC was part of an actionable conspiracy and performed a substantial act in furtherance of a conspiracy in Illinois."[16]

WDJ's Lawsuit

On April 27, 2004, the Wisconsin Department of Justice (WDJ) filed a civil lawsuit against Badger Die Casting and me claiming that the Wisconsin Department of Workforce Development had received complaints from former Badger Die Casting employees of unpaid medical bills. In their lawsuit, the state attempted to frame these unpaid medical bills as wages under Wisconsin Statute § 109.01(3) to get jurisdiction under Wisconsin State Law.[17]

Since the union had also filed its federal lawsuit and a complaint with the NLRB essentially making the same allegations, this was just another way for the union to exert more pressure on me to pay them what they were seeking. I again hired Mark Johnson with the law firm of Krukowski & Costello to represent me. In July 2004, since the union's healthcare claims were really a federal ERISA matter and not subject to state laws, my attorney had the case moved to federal court.[18]

In April 2006, without agreeing to any settlement, the State of Wisconsin requested that the court dismiss the lawsuit. And the court did just that. The whole thing had been another waste of taxpayer money.

DOL Sues Garrett

On September 7, 2004, the Department of Labor filed a civil lawsuit in federal court against me and my company, the Garrett Group, alleging that, from December 2001 through April 2002, I had "failed to segregate and remit the accounts so withheld into the [401(k)] plan's investment accounts" for Badger and that I had "failed to timely remit the amounts so withheld in the [401(k)] plan's investment accounts."[19]

These were the same allegations that had been brought against me in my criminal case involving Badger's 401(k) plan. Perhaps the government thought their criminal case was weak and they just wanted a backup plan. However, I still had to defend against this civil lawsuit because the allegations were wrong, since it had been Ron Bussan, Badger's controller, who had failed to make these payments. Since I had already been working with attorneys Bob Bartel and Mark Johnson with the law firm of Krukowski & Costello regarding Badger union matters, I decided to hire them to represent me in this case.

In May 2002, after Badger's business had already been closed for three months, I was first informed by Strong Funds via email that Badger had failed to pay the December 2001 401(k) contributions and had also failed to provide payroll data for the months of January 2002 though April 2002 so that Strong could determine what was due in employee 401(k) contributions.

I called Strong to say that while I was at Badger I had not been involved with transmitting payroll data or contributions to Strong and could not help with the payroll data they needed. I told Strong they needed to contact Ron Bussan who had possession of Badger's payroll records and who was now working for Randy Lubben at Wisconsin Die Casting. Strong's claim at the time just did not make sense. I was sure that Bussan had paid the December 2001 401(k) contributions to Strong since he had previously shown me evidence that he had wired in the 401(k) money.[20] I also would have assumed that someone from Strong would have contacted me if Bussan had not sent in the payroll data in early 2002.

Bussan had been Badger's controller since March 2000 leading up to the day Badger closed its business in April 2002. Bussan had been in charge of administering Badger's payroll and 401(k) plan. In particular, he was responsible for submitting employee payroll data to Strong each month so that Strong could determine the amount of employee contributions from payroll deductions and the amount Badger was to match. Bussan would then get an email from Strong each month indicating the amount Badger was to send in.

This was not the first time Bussan failed to send in payroll data to Strong. In fact, I had received an email from Strong in January 2002 informing me that Badger had not provided them with any payroll data for the months of September though December 2001 to determine what 401(k) contributions were due and had not paid over any 401(k) contributions.[21] At that time, I immediately met with Bussan to let him know about the email from Strong. Cash at Badger was tight, and since Bussan also handled Badger's cash flow and determined how much was available to pay creditors, I had assumed he decided to pay other creditors who had been providing more pressure. Nevertheless, that was no excuse. I told Bussan that, just like Badger's weekly payroll, he had to make sure the 401(k) contributions were paid on time—no exceptions. He assured me that he would get the payroll data and 401(k) contributions to Strong right away. I sent an email back to Preusker at Strong informing him that Badger would quickly get caught up on its past-due 401(k) contributions and that I had "also met with my staff at Badger to make corrective actions so that this will not happen again."

The following May, I was copied on an email from a woman at Strong to Ron Bussan informing him that she was now handling the Badger 401(k) account. She also let Bussan know that the last check received for December 2001 401(k) contributions had been returned by the bank and that Strong had not received payroll data for the months of January through April 2002. A few weeks later, Bussan dropped off the Badger's payroll data but only for the months of March and April 2002. The person at Strong sent Bussan an email and explained that Strong did not have the payroll data for January and February 2002. Bussan's assistant called Strong a couple weeks later to say she would be mailing in the January and February payroll data. Later that month, I was informed that Badger's unpaid 401(k) contributions were approximately $20,000. I again informed Strong that Bussan was responsible for the payment of Badger's 401(k) contributions and that Badger's assets were now in the possession of Lubben and Wisconsin Die Casting. I also explained that I did not have possession of these 401(k) funds to pay over. I told Strong they needed to contact Bussan for payment.

At that point, I had assumed that Badger's 401(k) plan trustee would legally pursue collections of these 401(k) contributions from Bussan or Lubben. I was not the plan fiduciary or plan administrator. UMB Bank was the trustee; Bussan was the fiduciary; and Badger was the plan administrator. I did not have possession of the 401(k) contributions to pay over and, short of litigation, could not force Lubben or Bussan to pay them over to Strong either. In fact, under federal law Lubben's company WDC was a "successor company," which meant that WDC was now responsible to see to it that these employee 401(k) contributions were paid over to Strong. Indeed, WDC had all Badger's cash and assets.[22]

By the time I learned of the DOL lawsuit regarding Badger's 401(k) plan in September 2004, I was up to my eyeballs in litigation, not to mention the criminal indictment that had been handed down just a few months earlier. After consultation with my attorney, we decided to ask the court to suspend, or "stay," this civil case pending the conclusion of my criminal case. After discussions with the DOL lawyers and their agreement to put this case on hold, my attorney filed a motion with the court at the end of March 2005, which the judge subsequently approved.[23]

After my criminal trial concluded in May 2005, the court lifted the stay in the civil case allowing the litigation with the DOL to continue. Since my other attorney, Bob Chapman, had been representing me in the union's federal lawsuit and had been doing an excellent job, I decided to have him take over the 401(k) lawsuit. After Chapman became acquainted with the case and I explained to him the details of Bussan's involvement, I told him that Bussan had been responsible for administering Badger's 401(k) plan, which included transmitting payroll data and paying over employees' 401(k) contributions to Strong.

Chapman decided not only to file an answer denying all the allegations put forth by the DOL against my company and me but also to file a lawsuit against Bussan.

DOL Sues Western

In September 2004, the DOL filed another civil lawsuit against me in federal court, this one related to Western Rubber. The DOL alleged that, in the month of June 2001 I had "withheld premiums from employees' paychecks and failed to remit the health premiums to Trustmark for the fully insured plan"; and that from July 2001 through February 2002, I "withheld employee health premiums from employees' paychecks and failed to remit them to the self-funded health plan for Western Rubber's payment of the claims."[24] Again, these were the same allegations that the government had brought in the criminal indictment. I again hired attorney Bob Chapman to defend me in this lawsuit. The case was put on hold until after my criminal case had been concluded.

In November 2007 we provided the DOL with detailed documentation demonstrating how the employee contributions were properly used toward Western's healthcare plan. Finally, almost two years later the DOL requested that the court dismiss the lawsuit. In September 2009, a federal judge did dismiss the lawsuit.[25] As it turned out, the DOL spent taxpayer's money and I spent several thousands of dollars over the course of five years defending what turned out to be a meritless and foolish lawsuit.

Chapter 10

Bad Defense

I AM SURE THERE ARE PLENTY of excellent defense lawyers out there who are extremely skilled, capable, thorough, and compassionate when it comes to representing clients faced with a federal criminal indictment and mostly likely prison time. Unfortunately, however, there are too many criminal defense attorneys who are inept and just in it for the money. These incompetent lawyers have managed to create for themselves a money-making scheme that involves charging a large flat fee and then feeding their clients to the federal prosecutors either by convincing them to plead out or spending very little time preparing their case for trial. Although such attorneys do file a few pre-trial boilerplate motions, they generally drag their feet in investigating the case with the hope that their client will just plead out before trial with devastating results.

In January 2004, my wife, Marie, and I met with my attorney, Stephen Glynn, and his partner, Michael Fitzgerald. As I mentioned earlier, Glynn had been written up in local magazines and newspapers over the years as one of the best criminal attorneys in southeastern Wisconsin. I had used him during the pre-indictment stage of my case. Glynn told us that Fitzgerald would be helping out with my case. Since I knew nothing about Fitzgerald's background or capability, I told Glynn that this would be fine as long as Glynn would be chief counsel; and Glynn acknowledged that this would be the case.

At that first meeting, we proceeded to discuss my case in some detail. I told them that I was innocent of the allegations made by the government and that I wanted to go to trial to prove my innocence. I stated that I was not interested in entering into any plea agreement with the government.

We then got down to discussing money. Fitzgerald said they would charge a retainer fee of $100,000 for preparing my case for trial and an additional fee would be required for the actual trial. I responded that I thought $100,000 was a lot of money and offered $50,000 instead. He said that my case would require a substantial amount of pretrial motions and investigation before trial so they would have to charge $100,000. I reluctantly agreed to the retainer amount.

In hiring attorneys Glynn and Fitzgerald, I understood they would thoroughly investigate my case as it related to the law, unearth evidence to be used to impeach government witnesses, and present such evidence to demonstrate my innocence at trial. The agreed-upon trial strategy, which I discussed with Fitzgerald, was that he would hire the necessary experts to analyze and present exculpatory evidence at trial, thereby alleviating the need for my testimony.

Investigation Procrastination

While I was indicted in January 2004, my arraignment was not held until the following month. At that time, the court scheduled my trial to start in the middle of May that same year. Since

I had not been involved in the day-to-day administration of the Badger Die Casting or Western Rubber healthcare and 401(k) plans, I was concerned about the accuracy of allegations made by the government with respect to employee funds not being properly used as outlined in the indictment. In March 2004, presumably to provide more time to investigate my case, Fitzgerald filed a motion with the court to move the trial date off. A new trial date was set for late September 2004. In early June 2004, I sent Fitzgerald an email stating that it had been over six weeks since we had spoken, my trial date was fast approaching, and that he needed to start investigating the government's witnesses and hire an accounting expert to audit Badger's and Western's books and records relating to my case. But instead, rather than hire the accounting expert, Fitzgerald had my trial date postponed for a second time until late February 2005.

In December, with the trial scheduled to start in less than ninety days, I sent Fitzgerald another email requesting that he hire an accounting firm to completely audit the health plans of Badger and Western to show exactly what had been deducted from these employee checks and what was paid to the respective benefits plans. Finally, a full year after I had retained his law firm, Fitzgerald got around to hiring Dick Ruffin and Michael Spang, two retired criminal investigation division agents with the Internal Revenue Service.

In mid-January, I received an email from Fitzgerald which stated, "I would like you to carry the ball on retrieving and storing the Badger records. They are your property and where you keep them and how much you spend is up to you . . . I would suggest Coakley Brothers. They store our closed files . . . Coordinate this with Dick Ruffin so he can start going through them as soon as they are available."

The Badger records were picked up from Wisconsin Die Casting and moved to Datastore (a Coakley Brothers company). However, the Western records were left at the Western plant in Goshen, Indiana. I later learned that this lack of "chain of custody" and safeguarding of this record evidence by Fitzgerald could have been real problem since these records might have easily been tampered with at Western or WDC.

Mock Trial

During one of our meetings, Fitzgerald brought up the idea of a mock trial. He explained that this would be a pretend trial in a staged courtroom at a local law firm in Milwaukee and would be a chance to see how I would handle a cross-examination and to test his defense. The law firm that had this mock courtroom would also provide randomly selected jurors. Fitzgerald said these mock trials were typically used in commercial litigation but not commonly in criminal cases and that this would be his first.

Present that day was another attorney, Rodney Cubbie, whom Fitzgerald had hired to play the role of prosecutor for the mock trial. Cubbie had been a prosecutor at the U.S. Attorney's Office in Milwaukee for several years and had left to go into private practice as a defense attorney. Fitzgerald also used a few of his office workers as government witnesses who were examined by both the mock prosecutor and Fitzgerald.

A visual aid used during this mock trial was a large poster-board that laid out the thirteen counts in the indictment, which Fitzgerald used in his opening statements. I gathered its purpose was to familiarize jurors with the counts brought by the government. But I thought that the posterboard actually did me a disservice, as it seemed to reinforce the specifics of the government's allegations rather than aid in my defense.

I did testify during this mock trial despite not having been prepared to do so beforehand. There did not appear to be any kind of organized defense that was tested with the mock jury, which seemed to me to be the whole purpose of the mock trial in the first place.

As it turned out, I ended up being convicted on several counts by the mock jury. This was not really a shock to me since none of the evidence demonstrating my innocence was ever presented. Fitzgerald simply cross-examined the two mock government witnesses without presenting any defense.

A few days later, we all got together and reviewed the videotapes of the jury deliberation. I noticed there were a few jurors strongly in favor of a conviction and others that were against it. There was some give-and-take among the jurors, and the ones with the strongest personalities won out.

More Delays, More Aggravation

Since nothing was really being done to properly investigate my case, I felt I had to personally get involved to help move things along. I reviewed Badger's records at Datastore and moved approximately ten banker boxes to my home in Brookfield, Wisconsin, for further evaluation. I met with Ruffin several times at my home to review these records. Ruffin eventually took possession of the boxes to aid in his evaluation.

In a February 2005 letter, I informed Fitzgerald that we had located evidence in Badger's records proving that in June 2001 employee payroll deductions were paid to United Healthcare and that Bussan had made an attempt to pay the 401(k) amount for January on two occasions. I also stated that there was still a lot of investigation yet to be done and requested that Fitzgerald complete the following tasks:

- audit the Badger health insurance premiums deducted from employees' checks and amounts paid to the health carrier;

- audit the Western health insurance premiums deducted from employees' checks and amounts paid to health carriers and check to see if Western employees paid the required forty percent of health premiums;

- have all the Western Rubber records moved to Milwaukee;

- hire a benefits attorney to evaluate Badger's 401(k) plan;

- get all details of 401(k) payments from Strong Funds;

- interview the government witnesses.

A few days later, Fitzgerald filed another motion with the court for my trial date to be moved off by sixty to ninety days. It was then tentatively set for mid-May 2005. Nevertheless, I was becoming more and more uneasy with each passing day and very concerned as to how, with time running out, Glynn would be able to get up to speed on my case in time for trial. I sent Fitzgerald an email stating that I wanted to meet with him and Glynn as soon as possible to discuss the work yet to be done before we commit ourselves to a new trial date.

The Attorney Switcheroo

A few days after I sent that email to Fitzgerald, I was told that Fitzgerald, not Glynn, would be representing me at trial. I had very little confidence in Fitzgerald's ability due to his continuing to push off my trial date and his failure to investigate the evidence surrounding my case. Besides, I did not know him to have any experience handling such a large and complicated case.

Both Marie and I were beginning to feel we had been swindled by the very attorneys we had hired to protect me from government prosecutors. Who was going to protect me from my own lawyer, and, with time running out, what was I going to do? I felt Fitzgerald had been deceiving us all along by telling us Glynn would be there as chief counsel. I did not trust Fitzgerald, but with very little time left to get a new attorney up to speed, I grudgingly decided to use him as chief counsel.

When I learned from Fitzgerald that Glynn was not going to be my trial counsel, Fitzgerald said, "Well, you can't make him represent you if he doesn't want to." Obviously my wife and I were shocked. We felt betrayed, misled, and defrauded.

I immediately called Fitzgerald and scheduled a meeting with both him and Glynn. Before the meeting, I sent a letter to Glynn laying out the entire situation and explaining why I felt mislead. I told him that if I had known from the beginning that he was not going to represent me, I would have interviewed other criminal attorneys and made my decision.

A few days later I received a written response from Attorney Glynn. He wrote:

> I received your earlier letter and had thought that a written response would not be necessary since we are meeting soon. However, because your letter raises a number of issues that need addressing, and in an effort to save some time at our meeting, I thought I should set these points out in writing and get them to you by fax and email before we meet.
>
> First, you hired our firm, not me personally. Had you hired me personally, I would have been the person

reviewing all the discovery, issuing subpoenas for additional documents, coordinating the investigation, attending court appearances, filing motions, writing briefs, preparing a mock trial, dealing with the prosecutors, and meeting with you on the number of occasions that Mike Fitzgerald has done all of these things.

Second, as you are aware, Mike has been acting as lead counsel in this case since last year when my brother's cancer situation took me away from the office on many and lengthy locations. Had you not found Mike's role as lead counsel acceptable, I would have expected you to raise this issue and let us address it. Since Mike, like me, is recognized in *Best Lawyers in America* as one of the few criminal law specialists in the state, and since he has also been recognized repeatedly in *Milwaukee* magazine as one of the best criminal lawyers in the city, and since he has probably tried more federal jury trials with retained clients than anyone else in the State of Wisconsin in the last two or three years, and since he has won a higher percentage of those trials than anyone else I know of in the private or public sector, I would have been surprised by your concern about him, but we could have addressed it.

Third, I first became aware of this being a problem when Mike told me that you were not interested in pursuing the government's offer that was, in my judgment, an extraordinarily reasonable offer that should have been accepted by you. It was, as a side point, substantially better than the offer the government was making when you and I appeared in the U.S. Attorney's office pre-indictment.

Glynn further stated in his letter:

If you wish to have this firm continue as your counsel, you will do so with Mike Fitzgerald as lead counsel and Craig Albee as research counsel. If that is not acceptable to you, I'm afraid you will have to act immediately to retain new counsel, and we will move to a withdraw. Given the fact that this case has already been adjourned a number of times, and the government made it clear that it would not agree to any further continuances, I think the likelihood of getting another trial date is extraordinarily slim. Thus, if new counsel is to be involved, they will have to be prepared to try this case on May 16th.

I was quite surprised by his letter, which was completely inconsistent with the prior sequence of events. First, I was unaware of any pre-indictment plea offer made by the government. Next, I had heard about the unfortunate situation regarding Glynn's brother, but was never informed by anyone that Fitzgerald had become lead counsel replacing Glynn. Instead, Fitzgerald kept assuring me that Glynn would be there until it was too late for me to find a different attorney. In fact, during our first meeting, Glynn specifically told my wife and me that he would be representing me at trial. Next, Michael Fitzgerald told my wife and me several times that Glynn would be representing me at trial and even commented that "he was a quick study" and not to worry. And finally, not only was Stephen Glynn's name on their initial retainer agreement under the signature line along with Michael Fitzgerald's, but it was also under the signature line on two pretrial motions filed with the federal court. And Glynn was the attorney of record.

After reading Glynn's letter, it became painfully clear to me what had happened. On the basis of Glynn's reputation, I was lured into his law firm. I was then sold on the fact that both Glynn and Fitzgerald would be working on my case. I was then charged the $100,000 retainer to cover all pretrial motions and the investigation of the case up to trial. Then Fitzgerald tried to convince me to plead out before trial which would have resulted in them keeping the $100,000 retainer fee without having to do all the legal work involved in a trial. That, I believe, explains why Fitzgerald did so little investigative work on my case until he realized I would not take the plea deal and was going to trial. Indeed, they counted on me pleading out before trial, which meant that Glynn's presence at trial would have become a non-issue.

I also realized that I was out of options. As Glynn stated in his letter, my case had already been adjourned several times, the government had made it clear that it would not agree to any further extensions, and there was little likelihood that the court would grant another trial date. Had I decided to hire a different lawyer, he or she would have had only a few weeks to prepare for the trial. This person would have had to start from scratch in investigating a very complex case. Unfortunately, this left me with no other reasonable choices but to continue with Fitzgerald and hope for the best.

For added protection, I decided to also retain Rodney Cubbie, the attorney who had participated in the mock trial, and whom I felt he had done a good job. While Cubbie didn't have the experience Glynn did, I hoped his involvement would help. I paid him a flat fee of $25,000.

Last-Minute Investigation

All of a sudden, with less than thirty days until the trial, Fitzgerald began investigating my case more seriously. He instructed Spang to travel down to the Western plant in Goshen to get the building key, interview witnesses, and investigate Western's evidence. After consultation with Fitzgerald, Spang brought back only a few Western records and left the rest there.

I was copied on an email from Fitzgerald to Ruffin that stated the following:

> One of the things we need to deal with is Steve's compensation through management fees charged to Badger and Western. I'm certain that the government will argue that it was excessive. We need to put Steve's compensation in perspective for the jury . . . I told Steve that he is free to work with you and Mike directly to produce charts, tables or graphs to illustrate this point. Again, the numbers have to be verifiable by you on the witness stand.

This was a critical email from Fitzgerald because this issue of my compensation is actually what *had* to be investigated and presented to the jury to rebut the prosecutor's claims. But as you will see later, this was never done.

Another email indicated that Spang was going to attempt to interview Bussan. However, I later learned that Bussan was on vacation and was never interviewed by the defense before trial.

All this sudden activity ordered by Fitzgerald to investigate and prepare with only a couple of weeks left before trial was very disconcerting, to say the least. I wondered why none of this had been done months earlier. Indeed, Fitzgerald, Ruffin, and Spang had had unrestricted access to Badger's and Western's records located at Datastore, at my home in Brookfield, and at the Western Plant. I was terrified that there really was not enough time left to get it all accomplished, let alone done right. Ten days before the trial, I sent Ruffin an email with a list of information that needed to be verified before the trial, including amounts deducted from Badger employee paychecks and over-payments made to United Healthcare; amounts deducted from Western employee paychecks and amounts for healthcare costs and expenses; and the amount of my actual compensation from Badger and Western.

Then unexpectedly, two days before trial, Fitzgerald informed me that he had decided not to put Ruffin on the stand to present my exculpatory evidence but instead would cross-examine government witnesses as his entire defense strategy. I was in shock, but his last-minute decision made sense because he was not prepared. What was interesting was that Ruffin had not been copied on this email, and I later found out that the day before the trial Ruffin visited the Datastore where Badger's records were kept and took with him a few banker boxes, perhaps in a desperate attempt to complete his work in time for trial.

If I had known this would be the outcome of my defense, I would have testified to present my evidence. However, now there was insufficient time to complete the investigation and prepare the necessary summary trial exhibits that I could have used at trial. I knew then that I was in big trouble but continued to hope for the best. What else could I do?

Plea Offer

From the beginning, I had been adamant about going to trial to demonstrate my innocence. Nevertheless, Fitzgerald was presented with the plea offer from prosecutor Gordon Giampietro in January 2005 and encouraged to persuade me to take it. This plea offer involved me settling the federal lawsuit brought by the Badger union for a cash payment of $400,000 and pleading guilty to one felony count. The government would agree to recommend a sentence of a year and a day, which meant that, according to federal sentencing guidelines, I would serve ten months in federal prison. Although my wife and I did consider this offer, it meant that I would have to stand before a federal court under oath and say that I committed a crime that I did not commit. This was something I was unwilling to do. I told Fitzgerald I would not accept the government's offer and that he needed to be prepared for trial.

Lesson Learned

If you are committed to going to trial, find a criminal lawyer who takes most of his or her cases to trial and wins many of them. Otherwise, you will be led down the road, as I was, thinking your lawyer is preparing for trial when he is really sitting on his hands preparing for you to take the best plea deal he can negotiate. If you end up on this dark, empty, confusing road, you won't stand a chance against your federal persecutors at trial.

Chapter 11

Trial By Deception

M Y TRIAL STARTED THE MORNING of May 16, 2005. The first order of business was jury selection or *voir dire*. There were approximately fifty potential jurors who had been sworn to tell the truth sitting in the courtroom all facing me, my two attorneys, and the two prosecutors. I sat with my two defense attorneys, Michael Fitzgerald and Rodney Cubbie, at one table; the two prosecutors who'd been assigned to the case, Assistant United States Attorney (AUSA) Gordon Giampietro and AUSA Matt Jacobs, sat at a different table.

I quickly found out that jury selection is hardly a selection at all. There was limited time, limited information, and, with my judge, limited effort to learn anything at all about the people who would be deciding my fate. In state court, jury selection can take days with the use of extensive questioners—but not in federal court. In federal court, you're almost guaranteed a jury ready to hear your case before lunch.

Both the government and my defense attorneys took turns striking out jurors. What troubled me was the fact that both the government and my attorneys seemed to be striking out the same types of people and seeking to retain highly educated professionals. It seemed that either my attorneys or the prosecutors had the wrong strategy in deciding what types of people would make the best jurors, and I hoped it wasn't my attorneys. Finally, almost by design, twelve jurors and two alternates had been selected by 11:04 A.M.—just in time for lunch.

Shortly after I had retained Glynn and Fitzgerald to represent me, Fitzgerald had told me that the judge assigned to my case, Judge Rudolph T. Randa, and the federal prosecutor Giampietro were friends. I asked him how he knew that, and Fitzgerald explained that they had been neighbors and socialized through various social and professional groups. I was immediately concerned and asked if this wasn't a conflict of interest. Fitzgerald told me that he had contemplated asking the judge to recuse himself but was concerned I might not fare so well with one of the other judges I could end up with. He said that Judge Randa was a "fair judge" and left it at that. We never did talk about this issue again since I assumed his decision not to ask for the judge's recusal was the best decision.

Wealth Evidence

Government prosecutors need to have a story—commonly called the "theory of the case"—about the motive of the crime they are prosecuting. The government voices this theory to the press, the trial court, the jury, and later, if necessary, to the appellate court. Their theory in my case was that employee funds did not get used as intended since I intentionally used their money for my company expenses and for my self personally.

Anticipating that the government would attempt to admit at trial irrelevant evidence as to my personal income and assets—

"wealth evidence"—in their attempt to prejudice me in front of the jury, Fitzgerald had filed before trial what is called a motion in limine. Basically, this motion requested that the court not allow this wealth evidence to be admitted at trial by the government since it was irrelevant to the charges in the indictment.

In response, AUSA Giampietro had filed a written opposition to our motion with the court claiming that this wealth evidence was relevant and that they needed it to show their theory of the case, which would prove criminal intent. Giampietro claimed this evidence would support his theory of my "systematic draining of funds from the companies—through exorbitant management fees and expenses—to support [my] lavish lifestyle [which] put the companies in a situation where [I] was prompted to, and did, convert the employee funds that are charged."[26]

Misleading the Court

The morning of the trial, there was a hearing before Judge Randa to determine whether this wealth evidence would be allowed. After hearing oral arguments by both sides, Judge Randa expressed concern over the government's use of this wealth evidence. For that reason, the judge indicated that his ruling would be preliminary since the nature of the evidence admitted during trial might later alter the court's decision.[27] Attempting to convince the court to allow admission of this wealth evidence now, Giampietro made the following statement as to why he needed to use this evidence immediately: "the theory of the government's case is . . . the Defendant withdrew significant amounts of money in management fees and other related expenses. And with those funds, used them to purchase significant assets, such that by the time 2001 rolled around, there was . . . insufficient funds in these businesses with which to honor his obligations, which are the subject of the indictment . . . It goes to the issue of motive and intent."[28]

Apparently persuaded by Giampietro's claims, Judge Randa changed his ruling and allowed this wealth evidence to be used by the government conditionally: the government was allowed to make their wealth evidence argument only during opening statements to the jury, and if they admitted evidence that supported their argument, they could make that same argument "subsequent," or later, to the jury during trial.[29]

The jury was then brought in and sworn in, and the trial was underway.

In its opening statement, the government proceeded to make its wealth evidence argument to the jury. Giampietro stated: "The evidence will show that [Mr. Whiting] acquired Badger Die and Western Rubber . . . [and] began withdrawing significant management fees . . . [and] used his management fees to fund the purchase of significant assets for . . . himself. Among some of those things were . . . a $700,000 condo in Florida, a $1.3 million home in Brookfield, and a $145,000 RV."[30]

Subsequently, one of my defense attorneys made his opening statement. Then it was time for each side to present their evidence called the "case-in-chief." The government went first.

During their case-in-chief, the government presented substantial amounts of wealth evidence to the jury such as the following:

- Government witnesses Bussan and DeSomer testified to payments made to me in compensation and expenses from Badger and Western.[31]

- Government witness DOL Investigator Archbold presented evidence of my personal aircraft purchases.[32]

- My personal financial statements showing my net worth were admitted.[33]

- My Franklin State Bank credit application for a mortgage was admitted.[34]

- A purchase contract for my Brookfield home was admitted.[35]

- Financial details of my home in Florida were admitted.[36]

- Lease payments paid by Western to WRA Holdings for rent was admitted.[37]

- Government witness FBI Agent Sparacino presented financial information of my personal RV.[38]

- Financial details relating to my company, Ace Precision Casting, was admitted.[39]

Then, during closing arguments to the jury, the government used this wealth evidence throughout their arguments. For example, the prosecutor stated that I "borrowed money from LaSalle Bank. [I] borrowed money from the sellers of Badger Die Company. Borrowed money from other entities and bought these companies . . . then [I] milked them for everything they were worth. [I] took all the money [I] could out of them, and to a point where [I] had to start taking money from the employees."[40]

But as it turned out, after all this wealth evidence was admitted and argued to the jury in a prejudicial way, the government never did show *any* evidence demonstrating that the money I received in compensation from either Badger or Western was ever used to purchase any of my personal assets. This was the case even though the government had assured Judge Randa it would do so to get the wealth evidence admitted in the first place. In fact, the government's own witness, FBI Agent Terry Sparacino, testified that he could not find "a single dollar of money deducted from employee paychecks for 401(k) contributions or healthcare premiums" that ended up in "Mr. Whiting's pocket."[41]

Judge Randa never said anything about this extraordinary violation by the government of his evidentiary ruling or even the misuse of the wealth evidence. In fact, neither of my defense attorneys ever brought this government misconduct to the court's attention or even asked the judge to strike this misused wealth evidence and deceptive government argument from jurors' consideration. As far as I was concerned, at the time, I had no idea about what was right and what was wrong and had put my faith in my attorneys that they would not let such misconduct by government prosecutors go unnoticed by the court.

Opening Statements

The primary purpose of an opening statement is to apprise the jury of the issues in question and to summarize the evidence that the parties intend to offer during the trial. The Supreme Court has characterized an opening statement as "ordinarily intended to do no more than to inform the jury in a general way of the nature of the action and defense so that they may better be prepared to understand the evidence."[42]

However, many unscrupulous federal prosecutors will use their opening statements as a way to influence the jury. "The prosecutor's opening statements should be an objective summary of the evidence reasonably expected to be produced [citation omitted], and the prosecutor should not use the opening statement as an opportunity to 'poison the jury's mind against the defendant.' "[43]

According to the *American Bar Association Standards for Criminal Justice: Prosecution Function* (3rd. ed.), prosecutors have a legal and ethical responsibility not to misuse opening statements.

> The prosecutor's opening statement should be confined to a statement of the issues in the case and the evidence the prosecutor intends to offer which the prosecutor believes in good faith will be available and admissible. A prosecutor should not allude to any evidence unless there is a good and reasonable basis for believing that such evidence will be tendered and admitted in evidence.[44]

In my case, one of the government's strategies was to use its opening statement to argue to jurors that in addition to the unpaid healthcare claims at Badger, I had failed to pay over $250,000 in healthcare claims for a Western Rubber employee named Dale Garber. Prosecutor Giampietro told jurors, "You will hear testimony from Dale Garber that his medical bills exceeded $250,000 and were never paid by Western Rubber at all."[45] At the time, I really had no idea whether Garber had this amount of unpaid healthcare claims or even if Western was responsible for payment. I had assumed that my defense attorneys had thoroughly investigated my case and were aware of the legitimacy, or lack thereof, regarding Garber's healthcare claims.

In fact, Garber never did testify at trial and yet the government continued to argue to the jury that Garber's unpaid healthcare claims were somehow my responsibility: "[Garber's] got a lot of problems . . . high medical bills"; "[Garber's] claims never get paid."[46] At a minimum, this undoubtedly added to the jury's dislike of me, which I believe helped the government win their case and conviction.

After trial, I personally looked into this matter and found something shocking and unbelievable. Dale Garber had left Western's employment at the end of May 2001, and the last healthcare contribution deducted from his weekly payroll check was during the payroll period ending June 3, 2001. This was the last weekly payment he made for his May 2001 health insurance coverage, and all his healthcare claims incurred in May 2001 were paid. Further investigation revealed that Garber made no COBRA payments after he left Western to continue his healthcare coverage after May 2001. Therefore, his coverage ended on May 30, 2001. Garber's unpaid healthcare claims that the government had made such an issue about to jurors at trial were all incurred after he had already left Western and were not Western's or my responsibility. And yet this evidence was not admitted at trial by my defense attorneys.

Getting Witnesses to Lie

There were two key witnesses my defense lawyers knew would testify for the government—both employees who had previously worked for me.

The first was Thresa Palkowski. Palkowski had been Badger's director of human relations from the time I first purchased Badger in July 1998 through the time it closed on April 16, 2002. Thresa was always professional and in my opinion had done an excellent job while working at Badger. I had only good things to say about her, and, in fact, I gave her an outstanding employment reference letter shortly after Badger closed. Her position at Badger included interviewing new plant employees, handling questions about employee benefits, and administering and handling any union complaints. My attorneys and I were fully aware that Palkowski had been interviewed by the Department of Labor and FBI earlier. We also were aware of the comments made during my meeting with the government, before my indictment, when they presented me with Palkowski's meeting notice indicating that she would testify that I told her to use the words "insurance carrier" in reference to the new self-funded healthcare plan.

First of all, I never told Palkowski to use the language "insurance carrier." Palkowski drafted and published this notice all by herself as she did with all other union notices. But the first time I heard that allegation in this meeting, I really did not understand the significance or the intention of the government in making that allegation until things unfolded.

In April 2005, Fitzgerald, Cubbie, and private investigator Michael Spang met with Palkowski to discuss my case. Spang's Investigation Report regarding this meeting noted the following information provided by Palkowski:

> In July 2001, [Badger] changed their employee health plan to a self-insured program based on the recommendation of Denise Linden of the Moral Company. Linden told Palkowski that [Badger] could save money relative to healthcare costs by changing to a self-insured plan. There had also been a history of "low claims" for employee health matters.
>
> The Administrator of the self-insured program was MBA in Madison. Greg Enes of Frank Haack & Associates negotiated with MBA on behalf of BDC. Frank Haack & Associates is a insurance brokerage

company. Enes at a meeting also discussed the change to the self-insured program with Whiting, Ron Bussan, and BDC Controller, and Palkowski.

Based on conversations Palkowski had with Whiting, he made it clear that he wanted to maintain the same level of healthcare, but at a lower cost. In part this decision was also based on the fact that BDC sales were lower than normal.

Also included in Spang's report was the following comment: "We showed Palkowski a memorandum notifying the [Badger] employees of the change to MBA. The memorandum was posted on at least three employee bulletin boards at [Badger]. Palkowski does not believe that the word "carrier" (versus "administrator") was misleading. She helped prepare at least part, if not all, of this memorandum. At no time did she feel that she was attempting to mislead or criminally hide the essential nature of the change to a self-insured plan. Also at no time did she feel that Whiting intended to mislead or criminally hide the nature of this planned change to the employees. Whiting never told Ms. Palkowski to mislead the [Badger] employees."

My trial lasted only five days, starting on Monday, May 16, 2005, and ending Friday morning, May 20. Palkowski, one of the government's key witnesses, was called to the stand on Tuesday at around four o'clock in the afternoon. The government started off by asking her basic questions such as her employment and education history. Then they proceeded into the details of her job responsibilities at Badger and details of Badger's health insurance programs.

My defense team and I both knew the government's purpose in having Palkowski testify was to support their "theory" that I had intended to mislead Badger union employees into thinking that their healthcare claims were completely covered by an insurance company rather than being covered by an insurance company only after Badger paid the first $30,000 in claims. They intended to prove this theory by making the jury think I directed Palkowski to use the term "insurance carrier" (rather than "insurance administrator") in the meeting notice.

Moreover, the government's theory was that despite the fact that it was Palkowski who wrote the draft, put her name on the bottom of the meeting notice, printed the notice, and then posted it for employees, I was the one who allegedly instructed her to use the language "MBA, our new insurance carrier" instead of "MBA, our new administrator," the language Palkowski, after much arm twisting, testified that she intended to use. This would support the government's arguments to the jury that they should convict me of a crime on counts 10 and 11.

What is even more ridiculous about this theory surrounding the "insurance carrier" wording is that the government was not required to show evidence that any Badger employee relied on it. In other words, the government was permitted to hatch this theory and convince a witness like Palkowski to twist the truth, and then was not required to provide testimony from even a single employee who believed MBA was an insurance company. This was a lucky break for the prosecutor, since all of the Badger employees had attended the sign-up sessions conducted by MBA personnel and were told that MBA was the administrator and not an insurance company.

In fact, presumably, for this government theory to be convincing to jurors, the government had to establish that I received a draft of this meeting notice *before* I allegedly instructed Palkowski to use the language "insurance carrier." Otherwise, if she prepared, signed, and posted this notice, then when would I have allegedly directed her to use such language? But as Palkowski's testimony unfolded, the government's coaching and influence over her testimony before trial became obvious.

During her testimony, when the government attempted to direct her down their chosen path, she testified she couldn't recall how the meeting notice was prepared and could not remember providing me with a draft of this notice beforehand. I am sure the prosecutor was very angry when that tidbit came out of her mouth. As I watched her being questioned, I could see terror and trepidation on her face. I remember thinking, *Just tell the truth, Thresa.*

The following exchange between the government and Palkowski took place:

Giampietro: Did Mr. Whiting ask you to prepare anything in anticipation of the enrollment meeting that was going to be held next week?

Palkowski: Yes. To post a notice.

Giampietro: And did he ask you to prepare that notice?

Palkowski: Yes.

Giampietro: And you did so?

Palkowski: Yes, I did.

Giampietro: And did you bring him back a draft of the notice that you had put together?

Palkowski: *I don't remember if there was a draft, or if I just read it to him over the phone. I don't remember . . . how it was prepared.*[47]

At this point, I thought Palkowski's testimony was clear: she could not remember if she made a draft of the meeting notice or how she even prepared it. However, absent any objection by my defense attorneys, the prosecutor continued to press Palkowski in an attempt to get the answer he wanted.

Giampietro: Okay, so to the best of your recollection, you weren't in the same building with him at Badger Die when you were drafting up this notice?

Palkowski: I don't . . . I believe that's correct.

Giampietro: You think . . . where would he have been?

Palkowski: I think I was at the plant, and I don't think Steven was in the building.

Giampietro: And at some point did you provide him, again, with a draft of what you were proposing to put up to the employees? How did you communicate to him what it is you put together?

Palkowski: Probably read it to him. Just read it to him. Or perhaps faxed it to wherever he was.

Giampietro: Whether you read it to him, or faxed it to him, Miss Palkowski, what did the notice that you . . . what did that notice indicate regarding MBA?

Palkowski: It indicates they're the insurance carrier.[48]

Now it's important to point out a key issue concerning how trial testimony is supposed to work. Palkowski had already been *asked* by the government if she provided me with a draft of the meeting notice before she published it, and she *answered*, "I don't remember if there was a draft or if I just read it to him over the phone," and "I don't remember how it was prepared." Once a witness has answered a question, especially the government's own witness, the prosecutor is not permitted to ask the same question again or to harass their own witness in hopes of getting the answer they desire. Once Giampietro asked Palkowski "[a]nd at some point did you provide him, *again*, with a draft of what you were proposing to put up to the employees?" one of my attorneys should have immediately stood up and objected by stating, "That question has been asked and answered." But instead they both just sat there.

Next, when asked by the prosecutor "[w]hether you read it to him, or faxed it to him, Miss Palkowski, what did the notice that you . . . what did that notice indicate regarding MBA?" and she answered, "It indicates they're the insurance carrier," that should have been the end of the allegation that I somehow instructed her to use the wording "insurance carrier" right then and there. But it wasn't. Shrewdly though, the prosecutor quickly responded, "Well, before we start talking about Exhibit 21, though, what did you advise Mr. Whiting your proposed notice was going to say about MBA? Again, it's not Exhibit 21."

Finally, after several more minutes of what amounted to a cross-examination by the prosecutor of their own witness, Palkowski finally caved in and said that I had instructed her when she was drafting the meeting notice to use the term "insurance carrier" rather than "administrator" even though she had initially testified that she didn't remember if there was even a draft or how it was prepared.

After the prosecutor was finished with his direct examination of Palkowski, it was our turn to cross-examine her. After some initial questions, Fitzgerald focused Palkowski's attention on the meeting she'd had with him a few months back.

The following exchange took place between the Fitzgerald and Palkowski:

Fitzgerald: And do you remember telling us in that meeting that you didn't feel that the word carrier was misleading or false? Do you remember telling us that?

Palkowski: I don't feel the intent was to mislead, no.

Fitzgerald: You don't. Alright. You don't feel . . . I mean, it's your testimony today that you don't believe that it was your intent or Mr. Whiting's intent to mislead the employees by using the word carrier, is that right?

Palkowski: That is correct.

Fitzgerald: And you told us that's because . . . for two reasons. Number one, because there was a carrier involved that was providing the stop-loss insurance, is that right?

Palkowski: Yes.

Fitzgerald: That's one of the reasons why you don't think the word is misleading, right?

Palkowski: Yes.

Fitzgerald: Because there was an insurance company as part of the package to provide insurance for claims above $30,000 per employee, is that right?

Palkowski: Yes.

Fitzgerald: And you also told us—and I assume it's your testimony on the stand today—that the other reason that you didn't think that there was anything wrong with using that word is it seemed less complicated or easier to explain the whole terminology of it to the employees.

Palkowski: Yes.[49]

After her testimony, I was convinced that the jury fully understood what had happened. That Palkowski had on her own drafted and posted the meeting notice to the Badger employees and that I had had nothing to do with the language she selected.

Also, the term "insurance carrier," which she had used to describe the MBA health insurance plan, was nothing more than her selection of wording and that neither she nor I ever intended to mislead or deceive the Badger employees.

Witness Intimidation

During Palkowski's cross-examination by Fitzgerald, something took place in the courtroom that I just couldn't believe. At the time Fitzgerald started questioning Palkowski about their interview at the restaurant and her statement that neither she nor I intended to mislead Badger employees regarding their healthcare, I had immediately noticed Giampietro, who happened to be sitting at the table just in front of me, leaning forward on the edge of his seat and staring her down. It was clear to me that he was attempting to send the message that Palkowski needed to stay on script . . . or else.

Immediately the expression on Palkowski's face changed from apprehension to sheer terror. At first, I just sat there amazed that what looked to me like blatant witness intimidation by a government prosecutor could actually be happening in open court in front of the judge and jury. I nudged Cubbie, who was sitting right next to me, and whispered to him what I saw happening. He said he had noticed it too.

I guess I was expecting him to stand up and announce to the court that the government was attempting to intimidate this witness, but he just sat there and did nothing. At the end of the day, we both mentioned this episode to Fitzgerald, who didn't seem surprised, but said, "I don't think the jury will appreciate it." After that incident, I quickly became convinced that the government was willing to do whatever it would take to win this case.

Closing Statements: A Story Without Evidence

According to ethics rules as outlined in the ABA Standards for Criminal Justice Prosecution Function, "In closing arguments to the jury, the prosecutor may argue all reasonable inferences from the evidence in the record. The prosecutor should not intentionally mis-state the evidence or mislead the jury as to the inferences it may draw."[50] The commentary section of this ethics rule pertaining to arguments to the jury state:

> The prosecutor's argument is likely to have significant persuasive force with the jury. Accordingly, the scope of the argument must be consistent with the evidence and marked by the fairness that should characterize all the prosecutor's conduct. Prosecutorial conduct in argument is a matter of special concern because of the possibility that the jury will give special weight to the prosecutor's arguments, not only because of the prestige associated with the prosecutor's office, but also because of the fact-finding facility presumably available to the office.[51]

Nevertheless, regardless of this ethics rule and the prosecutor's legal obligation to conduct a fair trial, many prosecutors still play by their own rule—to win at all costs. In my case, the federal prosecutors made several deliberate mis-statements of fact knowing that their arguments were not supported by any trial evidence in their hope of influencing the jury. Here are just a few examples:

- AUSA Matt Jacobs represented to the jury that "the evidence does show [Badger] took the money from the employees . . .

[and] *use[d] it to pay Mr. Whiting.*"[52] However, not only was there no evidence showing that any employee payroll deductions were paid to me, but the government's own witness, FBI Agent Terry Sparacino, testified that he could not find "one dollar" that was paid to me from employee payroll deductions.[53] As a result of this misconduct, Jacobs violated several ethics rules including the one that states "[t]he prosecutor should not intentionally mis-state the evidence or mislead the jury as to the inference it may draw."[54]

- During closing rebuttal arguments, AUSA Giampietro told the jury: "[y]ou have no idea whether . . . Mr. Whiting . . . had a personal guarantee on the loans to LaSalle [Bank]."[55] However, Ron Bussan had already testified that I had personally guaranteed the loans at LaSalle: "Mr. Whiting is the one who had guaranteed the loans to LaSalle Bank."[56] This was a deliberate attempt to mislead the jury.

- During his closing rebuttal argument, Giampietro told the jury that the idea that medical claims were going to be paid by the purchaser of Badger was "complete speculation on the record in this case" and that there was "no evidence of that."[57] However, the evidence in this case shows Giampietro's arguments to the jury were clearly false. Palkowski testified that "Whiting told [her] that he wanted to sell Badger to a buyer who would pay the unpaid medical claims" and that "Whiting told [her] if he did the deal with Mr. Lubben . . . it was [Mr. Whiting's] desire to have Lubben pay any unfunded medical claims."[58] Therefore, Giampietro again deliberately mis-stated the record in his attempt to mislead the jury.

- Giampietro, during his rebuttal closing arguments, told jurors that "[Mr. Whiting] made no mention of a plan to sell [Badger] to anybody, certainly not Randy Lubben."[59] However, this again is an intentional mis-statement of the facts in evidence. Palkowski testified that "Mr. Whiting . . . said that he was going to try to sell Badger" and that one potential buyer was "Randy Lubben."[60]

Convicted

On Friday May 20, 2010, at 11:00 A.M., the government rested its case. During a recess that morning, I sat down with my defense attorneys Fitzgerald and Cubbie. They were both positive about our case in that they thought the government had failed to present sufficient evidence to support the jury to convict me beyond reasonable doubt. Besides, there wasn't much we could do in presenting a defense. Fitzgerald, a few days before the start of trial, had decided not to put on a defense but to instead cross-examine government witnesses. I believe he made this decision because he was not adequately prepared for trial.

The defense and the government each made their closing arguments, and the jury started their deliberations at just after 4:00 P.M. on Friday.

Fitzgerald told the jury during closing that the government had to prove beyond a reasonable doubt that I had acted with intent to defraud. He said that intent to defraud in this case meant that "if the acts charged were done knowingly, with the intent to deceive or cheat another, in order to cause a gain of money or property to the defendant, or the loss of money or property to another, that's criminal intent."[61] This so happens to be the same intent instruction that the court gave jurors. Fitzgerald went on to discuss the evidence in the case, trying desperately to create reasonable doubt in the minds of the jurors, but as you will learn later in this book, reasonable doubt is a great textbook theory to be learned and debated in law schools but is a pretty obscure concept in the minds of jurors. It would have been much more effective if Fitzgerald had put on a defense using available exculpatory evidence to clearly demonstrate that all the government's fuzzy math and one-sided wealth evidence presentation was simply a farce.

The jury stopped deliberating when the court recessed at 5:30 but reconvened on Monday and had a verdict shortly after 3:00 P.M. later that day. The total time for deliberating my case was only around six hours.

After the week-long trial, I really wasn't sure what the verdict would be. When the jury finally entered the courtroom, I was stunned to hear it: *guilty on ten out of thirteen counts.*

I was found guilty on:

- Count 1: converting (stealing) $6,134 in Badger employee payroll deductions intended for Badger's healthcare plan.

- Counts 3 and 4: converting $10,270.23 in Western's employee payroll deductions intended for Western's healthcare plan. The government conceded at trial that the amount was not $39,281.00.[62]

- Counts 5, 6, 7, 8, and 9: converting $20,752 in Badger employee payroll deductions intended for the employees' 401(k) plan.

- Count 10: making an intentional false statement relating to the use of the wording "insurance carrier" in the meeting notice.

- Count 13: making a false statement relating to providing funding for Dale Garber's medical bills at Western.

I was acquitted on:

- Count 2: converting $6,761 in Badger employee payroll deductions intended for Badger's healthcare plan.

- Count 11: making an intentional false statement relating to the use of the wording "insurance carrier" in the plan-change notice.

- Count 12: making an intentional false statement related to a document titled "Funding of Health Claims for Badger Die Castings."

Needless to say, my wife and I were devastated. Here I stood convicted of stealing a total of $37,156.23, with criminal intent, in a business through which I had had access to millions of dollars in cash flow, millions in assets, and a 401(k) plan with $2 million in investments. I was shocked. There was absolutely no evidence that I had received any employee money. On what basis had the jury convicted me? This was my first glimpse of the power, influence, and persuasion federal prosecutors wield in front of the average juror in convicting the innocent. While driving home, I thought, *We are all at risk.*

The Evidence Against Me

So what evidence did the government present at trial to cause the jury to convict me of these crimes?

First, as it relates to Badger, the government alleged in the indictment that in June 2001, I misused $6,134 in funds deducted from employees' paychecks intended to be used for their June 2001 healthcare premiums.[63] The evidence prosecutors presented at trial were payroll records that showed $6,134 deducted from employee paychecks in June 2001 and testimony from a United Healthcare administrator that Badger had failed to make the June 2001 group healthcare payment to United. There was, however, evidence admitted that all employees' healthcare claims for June 2001 were paid by United. The government then argued to the jury that since the June 2001 group healthcare premium payment was never paid to United, this showed that these employees' deductions went elsewhere—namely, to me or to Badger. However, as you will learn later, my defense counsel failed to show the jury that on June 4, 2001, Badger in fact paid United $41,068,16, which included employees' June 2001 healthcare contributions of $6,134.[64]

Next, the government alleged in the indictment that from December 2001 through April 2002, Badger failed to pay over $20,752 in funds deducted from employees' payroll checks intended for their 401(k) plan.[65] The only evidence presented by prosecutors at trial were payroll records showing $20,752 was deducted from employee paychecks and testimony from Ron Bussan (Badger's controller) that I told him not to pay over these employee deductions to the 401(k) plan. In fact, other than Bussan's self-serving and mendacious testimony, there was not a shred of evidence that corroborated his story. The government then argued to the jury that since employees' 401(k) payments were never paid to the 401(k) plan, this demonstrated that these employee funds went elsewhere—again, to me or used by Badger. But as you will also learn later in this book, my defense counsel failed to impeach Bussan's testimony with available evidence and failed to show the jury evidence that it was Bussan, not I, who was responsible but failed to transmit these employee 401(k) contributions.[66]

In fact, as Badger's controller, Bussan managed the payroll and 401(k) calculations; sent the payroll data to Badger's 401(k) plan administrator, Strong Funds, so that they could calculate the amount due in employee contributions; received the invoice from Strong Funds exclusively via email indicating the amount of employee 401(k) due; and paid the employee 401(k) contributions to Strong Funds.

And lastly, the government alleged in the indictment that I caused Thresa Palkowski (Badger's human relations director) to use the language "insurance carrier" in a meeting notice provided to employees, knowing that such a statement was materially false.[67] The only evidence presented by prosecutors at trial was Palkowski's testimony that I instructed her to use the wording "insurance carrier"; there was no other evidence admitted at trial to corroborate her story. The government then argued to the jury that I had intended to mislead the employees into thinking that the MBA healthcare plan was insured entirely by an insurance company. But my defense counsel failed to put his investigator, Mike Spang, on the stand to testify about his interview of Palkowski before trial in which she stated that she did not believe that her wording "carrier" was misleading; she helped prepare at least part, if not all, of this meeting notice; at no time did she feel that I intended to mislead or criminally hide the nature of the new healthcare plan; and I "never told her to mislead the Badger employees."[68] In addition, as you will learn later, after trial, Palkowski recanted her trial testimony that she, not I, selected the language "insurance carrier" used in the meeting notice.[69]

Now I will discuss the evidence presented by the government relating to Western Rubber. The government alleged in the indictment that from June 2001 through February 2002, I misused $39,231 in funds deducted from employees' paychecks intended to be used for their healthcare plan.[70] The government later conceded at trial that the amount allegedly converted was only $10,270.23. The evidence prosecutors presented at trial were payroll records showing that $44,543.01 was deducted from employee paychecks from June 2001 through February 2002 and the testimony of a government investigator—using his summary exhibit—that Western only paid out $34,272.87 in healthcare benefits, insurance premiums, and administration costs to the plan administrator.[71] The government then argued to the jury that since Western did not use all employee payroll deductions toward the healthcare plan, that I, for the benefit of myself or Western, misused the difference of $10,270.23. However, as you will learn later in this book, my defense counsel failed to investigate available evidence and show the jury the correct accounting of Western's healthcare plan. From April 2001 though February 2002, Western collected $59,078.73 from employees' payroll deductions and paid out $100,832.89 in healthcare benefits, insurance premiums, and administration costs to the plan administrator. This demonstrates that Western paid out $41,754.16 more in healthcare expenses then it received from employees.[72]

And finally, the government alleged in the indictment that I made a material false statement when I told the controller and general manager that I had a plan to provide funding for the cancer treatments of a Western employee named Dale Garber.[73] The only evidence prosecutors presented at trial relating to this allegation was the testimony of Alan DeSomer (Western's controller) who said that "we were going to pursue an additional policy to cover that claim at a higher level than the other group of employees" and the testimony of Phil Hamilton (Western's general manager) who said, "I believe there was mention of a . . . maybe a separate insurance policy to be taken out on [Garber] to cover that situation."[74] The government then argued to the jury that my statement of a plan to pay Garber's unpaid healthcare claims, which I allegedly knew was false, had been relied on by the controller and general manager. However, as you will learn later, my defense counsel failed to investigate and present such evidence to the jury that Garber was not even an employee of Western at the time he incurred the unpaid healthcare claims referred to by the government and had failed to pay his COBRA premiums to continue his health insurance. Further, that my defense counsel failed to investigate and present evidence to the jury that any Garber healthcare claims legally due to be paid by Western would be paid out of the Western asset sale proceeds.[75]

Next, even if employee money did not end up where it was supposed to doesn't necessary mean that I committed a crime. Prosecutors have to show that I had a "culpable mind" or deliberately intended to steal employee money rather than as a result of an accident or by oversight. This is where the government prosecutors are really good at trickery and illusion. The evidence they admitted in this regard is what is referred to as "wealth evidence." First, the government admitted copies of all payments made to me from Badger and Western; but, of course, they failed to state the fact that the purpose of these payments was to offset amounts I personally put into these company out of my own pocket. Presenting this fact was the responsibility of my defense attorneys. Next, they admitted evidence that I owned two houses, an airplane, and an RV. Then they argued to the jury that I had absolutely no risk in owning Badger and Western and that I had "looted" my companies by stealing employee payroll deductions totaling $37,156.23 ($26,886.00 from Badger and $10,270.23 from Western).

However, as you will learn, my defense counsel failed to investigate and present evidence to the jury that my net compensation as Badger's CEO and president was only $110,000 per year and my average compensation as Western CEO and president was only $170,000—well below the industry norm. They also failed to investigate and present to the jury that I had $10 million of personal risk that included personal guarantees, investments, and loans to these companies.[76]

As the facts of my case clearly demonstrate, there are a couple of important points here. First, a federal criminal trial really has very little to do with the actual facts or whether or not someone is actually guilty or innocent of the allegations made. And second, without a proper defense, you don't stand a chance against a prosecutor whose ambition is to win rather than to do justice.

Even though I was found guilty of intentionally violating federal criminal laws, I know I did nothing wrong and have set out to prove my innocence and get justice.

Chapter 12

Suing Bussan

A FTER THAT DEVASTATING VERDICT, I was very disappointed in our federal criminal justice system. But I was more disappointed by Bussan and Palkowski, who were willing to throw me under the bus by lying to protect what they perhaps perceived to be their illegal conduct.

While I can certainly understand that anyone who is interviewed by the FBI or federal prosecutors is likely scared and maybe even terrified, that is no justification to lie. As it turned out, Palkowski unintentionally used the wording "insurance carrier" in the meeting notice she published and Bussan decided to pay off other Badger vendors instead of the 401(k) contributions to keep Badger open. None of their conduct was criminal under the circumstances.

All they had to do was tell the truth and, if I was interviewed by the government, I would have also told them that they did nothing wrong and certainly nothing intentionally illegal. Badger's underfunded healthcare and 401(k) claims still would have been settled civilly, as they were, without all of this devastation.

In July 2006, in responding to the DOL's lawsuit regarding Badger's 401(k) plan, my attorney Bob Chapman filed both an answer to the DOL's allegations and a lawsuit against Bussan with the federal court.[77] My attorney denied all the allegations made by the DOL made in the lawsuit.

Bussan was served with this lawsuit shortly thereafter. In our answer, we stated that Bussan was responsible for providing Strong with Badger's payroll data and 401(k) contributions. We also alleged that he failed to provide timely payroll data and to account for and pay over the Badger employee 401(k) contributions to Strong without my knowledge or consent. In gathering the evidence to support our allegations against Bussan, Chapman had conducted a deposition of Bussan the previous August. Based on Bussan's sworn deposition testimony, including other document evidence uncovered, Chapman presented the following facts, which were stated in the complaint against Bussan. Here is the summary:

> As Badger's controller, Bussan assembled and communicated payroll data to the 401(k) plan administrator, Strong Funds, and disbursed the applicable amount of payroll withholdings and employer contributions to the 401(k) plan. In late 2001, Badger fell behind in funding the 401(k) plan with Strong. In early 2002, Whiting learned of this problem and directed Bussan to send Strong the delinquent contributions. Bussan prepared a check for the delinquent 401(k) contributions, but that check was returned by LaSalle after Bussan and LaSalle discussed the matter without Whiting's knowledge or consent.

After learning of the returned check, Whiting instructed Bussan to wire the delinquent contributions to Strong, and Bussan prepared that wire. However, the wire was not honored by Badger's lender, after consultation between the lender and Bussan, and without Whiting's knowledge or consent. From January 2002 to April 2002, Bussan never provided Strong the payroll data needed to calculate the 401(k) plan contributions, interfering with Whiting or Strong's ability to determine what contributions might be due to the 401(k) plan. In fact, Bussan never provided this payroll data to Strong until June 2002, well after Badger had ceased operations and Badger's assets were transferred to Wisconsin Die Castings (WDC) by LaSalle Bank for whom Bussan immediately assumed the same position as controller. Funds necessary to pay the 401(k) contributions were available to Bussan during these months at Badger but Bussan, unbeknownst to Whiting, never provided the payroll data to Strong and, as a result, the 401(k) contributions were not paid to Strong, and the assets representing those contributions were transferred to WDC.

After I filed my answer and the lawsuit against Bussan, Chapman advised me that I should settle the case with the DOL but continue to pursue my lawsuit against Bussan. As he explained it to me, this would involve me paying an amount equal to the underfunded employee 401(k) contributions. Up to that point, I was really adamant about not paying anything relating to Badger. As explained earlier, Lubben had caused Badger to go out of business when he took over its assets and customers and proceeded to hire Badger's employees. However, as a matter of law, his company was responsible to pay the Badger employee 401(k) contributions to Strong Funds. There are federal laws to protect employees from individuals or companies who purchase assets of a business without first paying for employees' ERISA benefits.[78]

In addition, it sure appeared to me that Bussan and Lubben had been working together before Lubben took over Badger. Since about the time Lubben had started showing an interest in purchasing Badger, unbeknownst to me, Bussan suddenly stopped sending in Badger's payroll data to Strong—data that he routinely sent to Strong each month. If Strong didn't have Badger's payroll data, it could not determine the amount it needed to invoice Bussan for and as such would be unable to alert me that Bussan was not paying over employee's 401(k) contributions. Since Bussan became Lubben's controller the same day Lubben purchased Badger's assets, it stands to reason that Bussan knew Lubben's intentions weeks earlier. By not using Badger's assets to fund the approximately $21,000 of employee 401(k) contributions, Bussan enabled Lubben to receive $21,000 more in Badger's assets at closing. This allowed Bussan to garner an advantage with his new employer Lubben through what was essentially a $21,000 gift.

I had dug in my heels long ago and was not going to pay anything to anybody, but now my attorney was telling me that I should settle. On the other hand, I had already spent substantially more in legal fees than what the DOL was looking for and there were more legal fees to come. After a few days, I agreed to settle this case with the DOL only if I was not required to admit that I had done anything wrong and was still able to pursue my lawsuit against Bussan.

I guess, looking back, that this was somewhat of a strange request since I had already been convicted in May 2005 of personally misusing these same 401(k) contributions, but I knew that I would keep fighting in my criminal case for justice and the opportunity to prove my innocence. I called up my attorney and said, "Bob, let's settle the DOL case."

On October 31, 2007, I signed a settlement agreement with the DOL, without admitting the DOL allegations, and paid $26,617.01 that the DOL alleged was due to the 401(k) plan. I also paid approximately $10,000 for additional accounting fees and a fine to the DOL. The DOL agreed in this settlement to permit me and/or the Garrett Group, to pursue any third-party claims against any individuals or entities other than the Secretary of Labor for matters related to this lawsuit.

Once I settled my case with the DOL regarding Badger's 401(k) plan, I continued to aggressively pursue my lawsuit against Bussan. But surprisingly, he never filed an answer. At that point, I assumed that perhaps Bussan realized fighting this lawsuit was pointless. He had to know that his deposition testimony, in which he had said *he* would decide who would get paid at Badger to keep the doors open, was materially different than what he had testified to during my criminal trial. At that time, he had said that *I* had decided exclusively who got paid, which then allowed the government to argue to the jury that *I* had chosen not to pay the 401(k) contributions. At that point, he had committed perjury for the government. Maybe he just didn't want to dig his hole any deeper.

In February 2009, my attorney filed a default judgment with the federal court against Bussan in the amount of $35,940.41, and we proceeded against his personal assets.[79] Bussan hired an attorney, and they offered me $25,000 to settle the judgment.

Rather than spend more money on legal fees attempting to collect the judgment, I took his $25,000 offer and had my attorney file a "satisfaction of judgment" on July 17, 2009.[80] Also, as a matter of law, our allegations in the lawsuit against Bussan were now legally admitted facts.

All in all, I got what I wanted—payment from Bussan of Badger employees' 401(k) contributions and Bussan's admissions that he, not I, was responsible for paying over employees' 401(k) contributions to Strong. Nevertheless, as of the writing of this book, I still stand criminally convicted of converting these 401(k) contributions even though the evidence clearly shows otherwise.

Chapter 13

Federal Punishment

ONCE YOU HAVE THE MISFORTUNE of being convicted of a crime in our federal system, either by your own admissions or through a trial verdict, you will quickly learn that the process of indictment to imprisonment is lengthy and the consequences are draconian.

The process starts out with a thorough examination of your family, your background, and your finances by the U.S. Probation Office and then a battle between the government and your attorney over what your punishment should be. In approximately eighty-five percent of cases, this all ends with you waking up one day in a federal prison.

Then, if you decided to exercise your constitutional right to a trial rather than streamlining the prosecutor's job by pleading out, you can expect the prosecutor to teach you a lesson and fight for an even a longer sentence. In fact, once you are indicted, since no one in our federal criminal justice system likes a "fighter," you can expect to pay dearly if your journey results in a conviction.

Pre-Sentence Report

A pre-sentence report, also called a pre-sentencing investigation (PSI), is an investigation conducted by the U.S. Probation Office designed to provide additional information about a defendant that can be used by the judge when determining an appropriate sentence. The purpose of the pre-sentence investigation is to generate a complete profile of the offender. It includes basic demographic information along with interviews from the offender, family members, and other people who have come into contact with the offender. Pre-sentencing investigations can also go into things like prior convictions, medical and physical history, victim-impact statements, restitution, and so forth. Any information that could shed light on the offender in possibly demonstrating that mitigating circumstances were involved can be included. In addition, there is a section called "The Offense Conduct," which is basically a narrative put forth by the government prosecutor and used by the probation officer who writes the PSI report.

With the conviction and sentencing guidelines in mind, a judge reads through the pre-sentence investigation and considers this information when deciding which sentence would be most appropriate. There may be evidence that would lead to leniency or evidence that would suggest a harsher sentence. Pre-sentence investigation reports are also utilized to decide which prison facility would be most appropriate for the offender, based on the crime and the personal history.

My pre-sentence investigation started shortly after my conviction. I was interviewed by the U.S. Probation Office and assigned a probation officer. During the interview, I was questioned about where I lived, prior residences, education history, my family members, and details about my income including assets and liabilities, and was provided with a financial disclosure form that I had to complete with exhibits. It goes without saying I took great care in completing this form knowing full well that the prosecutor might go through it with a fine-tooth comb looking for something to use against me at a later date.

Once my PSI report was completed by the Probation Office, a copy was sent to the government and to my attorney. Each respective party then had the opportunity to respond to any inaccuracies they claimed were in the report.

Statement of Events

As part of the procedure in gathering the necessary background information about the crime, the probation officer who is writing the PSI report receives what is called the "Prosecution Version of the Events" from the prosecutor. This document is nothing more than the government stating its version of what it believed happened. In turn, the defense gets to respond to the government's report to the probation officer.

Keep in mind that once you are convicted of a crime in the federal system, nobody, least of all the probation officer who is writing your report, wants to hear about your claim of innocence, and making such a claim could have an adverse effect on your sentence. This is due to the fact that the probation officer's final sentence recommendation will undoubtedly impact the judge's sentencing decision.

In my case, the prosecutor's version of the events was simply the same fictitious story that was presented in the indictment and related to the jury at trial. Nevertheless, Giampietro's version was pretty much recited word-for-word in my PSI report for the sentencing judge to read. The only thing mentioned about my version of events in this PSI report was the following statement: "The defendant, through his attorney, indicates he maintains his innocence and plans on appealing this conviction."

Increasing My Sentence

In January 2002, Giampietro filed a motion with the court requesting access to my financial disclosure form and other supporting documents that I had filed with the U.S. Probation Office. It was clear to me and my attorney that Giampietro was on a fishing expedition to find anything he could to incite the judge against me to have an impact on my sentence. In his motion, Giampietro stated that "[f]inancial information provided to the Probation Department by the defendant . . . appears to be materially inconsistent with information the United States developed during pre-trial investigation and more recently in anticipation of sentencing," and as such he wanted the court to grant him full access to my complete file.

Also in this motion, Giampietro laid out—incorrectly I might add—several alleged areas in which he claimed I had attempted to mislead the Probation Office as to my assets and liabilities. It was clear that if Giampietro was successful in convincing the court that I had engaged in this kind of obstruction, the court would most likely increase my sentence. In anticipation of this, my attorney provided the court before my sentencing hearing with all the evidence demonstrating that Giampietro's allegations regarding my financial disclosure form were false.

Court-Ordered Sentence

Sentence calculation in the federal criminal justice system is considerably different than that in the state criminal system. Before the law was changed by the Supreme Court ruling *United*

States v. Booker, all courts had to follow federal sentencing guidelines for the sake of consistency.

Sentence calculations are conducted by the U.S. Probation Office after they have received input from both the government and the defense. A sentence recommendation and the basis for its determination are included in the PSI report for the judge to review before sentencing. It used to be that the court would verify this calculation to determine a sentencing range in terms of months. The court would then pronounce the sentence within this range and remand the convicted defendant into the custody of the Federal Bureau of Prisons.

However, after the Supreme Court ruling in *Booker*, the procedure changed significantly. Now, the sentencing guidelines are still calculated by the U.S. Probation Office and included in the PSI report but they are only "advisory" to the court. The court can sentence the defendant to a prison term that is longer or shorter than the guideline calculation based on either mitigating or aggravating circumstances of the case.

In my case, this change in law happened before my trial and I knew that if I was, God forbid, convicted, the judge could possibly sentence me to a much lower sentence than what the sentencing guideline had called for.

Initially, my sentencing was set for September 2005. However, due to the exchange of documents and the filing of several reports and motions with the court, I was not sentenced until February 2006. I really didn't know what to expect. But I did realize that sentencing under the federal criminal justice system tended to be draconian, with lengthy sentences handed out for conduct considered minor under state law.

The government was asking for a seventy-eight month prison sentence, while my attorney was requesting a twenty-one to twenty-seven month sentence which was within the advisory guidelines.

I arrived early to the courthouse with Marie. Several members of my family also came to provide support. Upon entering the courtroom, I first noticed a few Badger union employees sitting on the right side of the courtroom. Standing in the back was FBI Agent Sparciano and DOL Agent Archbold. Both had grins on their faces. Fitzgerald was at the defense table preparing his notes.

The first order of business related to the government's claim that I had provided inaccurate information on my financial disclosure form to the Probation Office. The prosecutor requested that the court add two guideline points for my alleged obstruction of justice, which would have increased my sentence. After Judge Randa heard all the evidence and arguments by both sides, he ruled against the government on this enhancement.

Next, the court heard statements from certain Badger employees who were apparently selected by the prosecutor as individuals who had been victimized by my alleged crimes. Being victimized by anyone is a serious matter and I don't want to appear to be insensitive to anyone who has truly been a victim of a crime, but I have to say that Giampietro's use of certain Badger employees during my sentencing before Judge Randa was shameful and appalling to say the least.

There were two sets of dynamics at play during my sentencing. The first was that the prosecutor was looking to get the longest sentence and largest restitution amount possible to enhance his standing. And the second was that a small group of Badger union employees were looking to convince the judge to increase the restitution amount as much as possible for their own personal benefit. In fact, as it turned out, all the statements made by these

Badger employees, and embellished by Giampietro, during my sentencing hearing were related only to Badger's underfunded healthcare claims—something that I was not even charged with.

Fitzgerald actually had to argue that I should be sentenced only for what the jury had convicted me of, which computed to a twenty-one to twenty-seven month sentence and restitution of $66,117, according to the sentencing guideline calculation. *My own attorney* never grasped that the amount was really $37,156.23 since the government conceded at trial that counts 3 and 4 were incorrect.[81] I had already provided Fitzgerald with the proper numbers. Giampietro argued to the judge that the underfunded healthcare claims of Badger employees and Dale Garber (a Western Rubber employee) were really part of the same crime. In particular, Giampietro argued to Judge Randa that the unpaid Badger employee healthcare claims (which had somehow mysteriously grown to over $500,000 from around $400,000 at trial) and the unpaid claims from Garber (alleged now to be $356,000) were really caused by certain false statement counts for which I was convicted. In spite of my attorney's vigorous objections, Judge Randa agreed with Giampietro and increased my sentence by sixty-three months and my restitution by $856,758 even though Giampietro assured the jury during trial that the unpaid healthcare claims were not part of the alleged crime.[82]

As it turned out, Judge Randa sentenced me to ninety months of incarceration—*more than three times as many* months as what was recommended for the crime for which I'd been convicted—and ordered me to pay $922,875 in restitution, $856,758 more than the amount the jury found me guilty of having "converted." This sentence also included three years of supervised release, which is similar to probation.

Although I was surprised by the judge's ruling, I knew that I would appeal both the conviction and the sentence and was very hopeful that the appellate court would make things right.

Attempting to Remain Free

Not having a great deal of confidence in the defense team that had represented me at trial and sentencing or that the outcome of my trial would result in a complete acquittal, early on, even before trial, I had set out on a search for the best appellate attorney I could afford. In doing research, it became clear to me that good trial attorneys and appellate attorneys have two different skill sets. Trial attorneys are good in court. Appellate attorneys are good writers of briefs, which is the core of the appellate process.

After talking with several people and checking around, I came up with the name Joel Bertocchi with the law firm of Mayer Brown in Chicago. Joel is an experienced criminal and appellate litigator who served as solicitor general for the State of Illinois and was a federal prosecutor handling numerous complex appeals on behalf of the government in addition to presenting cases before the Supreme Court. I felt his experience was perfect for my appeal in the event I was convicted at trial.

Bertocchi was present at my sentencing hearing and was ready to inform the court of my intentions to appeal both the conviction and sentence.

Meanwhile, Fitzgerald had informed me before sentencing that Giampietro would most likely request that I be handcuffed, shackled, and taken away right after sentencing; however, before this issue even came up, Bertocchi announced to the court that he would be filing a motion with Judge Randa requesting that I be permitted to remain free pending my appeal. Judge Randa provided approximately two weeks so that both Bertocchi and

Giampietro could provide briefs to the court arguing their respective positions. That quick thinking on Bertocchi's part saved me from having to spend many weeks locked up in some local state jail pending my transportation to a federal prison.

As expected, Judge Randa denied my request to remain free pending my appeal. Bertocchi's next move was to appeal Randa's decision to the Seventh Circuit Court. Courts of appeals decide appeals from district courts within their federal judicial circuits. Since my trial and sentencing had been conducted in the U.S. District Court of the Eastern District of Wisconsin, the Seventh Circuit Court out of Chicago would be hearing all of my appeals. Bertocchi filed an emergency appeal with the Seventh Circuit Court requesting that I remain free pending my appeal.

On Sunday, April 23, 2006, one day before I was to report to federal prison, I received word that the appellate court had denied my request to remain free pending the outcome of my appeal.

Off to Prison

All individuals who are convicted of violating a federal criminal law and who are sentenced to incarceration by a federal court end up under the jurisdiction of the Federal Bureau of Prisons (BOP), a subdivision of the U.S. *Department of Justice* responsible for the administration of the federal *prison* system. Although during sentencing my attorney requested that Judge Randa designate that I serve my sentence at the federal prison camp in Oxford, Wisconsin (about two hours from my home), so that my family could visit, I understood there was no guarantee I would end up there since the BOP sends you to a facility of their choosing

The BOP uses a point system that includes your age, prior convictions, history of violence, and general information in your

PSI. On the basis of this information and the points you receive, you are assigned to a low-, medium- or high-security prison facility. A low designation might mean a prison camp and a high designation would mean a federal penitentiary.

In late March 2006, I received a letter from my probation officer that I would be serving my time at a prison camp in Duluth, Minnesota, seven hours from my home, and that I needed to surrender myself there on April 24, 2006 by 1:00 P.M. I was very disappointed in the news. I called my defense attorney, and he said there was not much he could do about it.

On the morning of April 24, 2006, Marie and a friend of mine drove me up to Duluth for the start of my prison sentence.

Chapter 14

Relief By Appeal

B ECAUSE THE COURT OF APPEALS have only appellate jurisdiction, they do not hold trials. As such, appellate courts review decisions of the trial court for errors of law and only consider the record (papers the parties filed, transcripts, and exhibits from the trial) from the trial court and the legal arguments of the parties.

Once I was educated on how the appeals courts operate, I suddenly realized that *all the evidence that would demonstrate my innocence would not be reviewed by the appellate court since it had not been admitted by my attorney at trial and was not in the record*. Unfortunately for the innocent, that's just the way it works in this country. If there is evidence that was not presented at trial by your trial lawyer and he is found deficient by a federal court for not doing so, and that evidence more likely than not would have resulted in an acquittal, then the defendant just has to wait (in most all cases while incarcerated) until he or she has exhausted this direct appeal. Then, he or she can file a motion for a new trial pursuant to 29 U.S.C.§ 2255. (Later, I will discuss what a defendant can do in an attempt to overturn a conviction based on ineffective assistance of counsel.)[83]

My lawyer and I were limited to whatever evidence had ended up in the record. Since my appeal would involve issues that took place both at trial and during sentencing, Bertocchi would not be able to start reviewing the records until after my sentencing hearing. Also before he could start, he needed to get all of the trial and sentencing transcripts, including all of the exhibits admitted in my case. Since I was to report on April 24, 2006 to start my prison sentence, all of my communications with my appellate attorney had to be done through the mail and over the prison telephones.

In May 2006, I received the first draft of my appeal. I spent several days in the prison law library researching the issues addressed in the appeal. The jury had convicted me on ten of the thirteen counts in the indictment. Regarding the charges relating to Badger Die Casting: Count 1 had alleged that I converted $6,134 of employee funds deducted from their paychecks intended to be used for their health insurance premiums; counts 5 to 9 alleged that I had converted $20,752 of employee funds deducted from their paychecks intended to be used for their 401(k) contributions; and count 10 alleged that I made a false statement relating to Badger's health insurance program. As it related to Western Rubber: counts 3 and 4 alleged that I converted $39,231 of employee funds deducted from their paychecks intended to be used for their health insurance premiums; and Count 13 alleged that I made a false statement relating to the health insurance of a Western Rubber employee, Dale Garber.

However, for an individual to be found guilty of a crime under the federal statutes for which I was charged (18 U.S.C. §§ 664, 669), as it related to the count involving the conversion of money (counts 1, 3, 4, 5–9), the government had to prove beyond a reasonable doubt that the money in question was first subject to federal ERISA laws (Employee Retirement Income Security Act) and that I had "knowingly and willfully" intended to convert employees' money for my benefit or the benefit of someone else.[84] In other words, it was required that the government prove beyond a reasonable doubt that I took employee money totaling $66,117 with criminal intent.

The first issue of my appeal was whether or not the charges relating to counts 1, 3 and 5–9 were even a crime under the federal statutes for which I was charged. Bertocchi argued that the amounts deducted from employees' paychecks in these counts were not "plan assets" until they were paid over to the relevant ERISA plans and that these funds were merely a debt owed to the employees by Badger and Western subject to the terms of both companies' union agreements.[85] The issue of whether or not money deducted from employee paychecks that had not yet been delivered to an ERISA plan were subject to criminal penalties had not yet been ruled on by the Seventh Circuit Court.

The next was whether there was sufficient evidence presented at trial for the jury to convict me on counts 1 and 5–9. As to count 1, which related to employees' health insurance for the month of June 2001, in accordance with the union contract, Badger was required to provide employees with health insurance, and as Bertocchi stated in his brief, "United covered Badger employees' medical claims for June 2001."[86]

Bertocchi further argued:

> As for the use of employee deductions, Badger's healthcare related expenditures far exceeded the amounts deducted from Badger employee paychecks. Between June 2001 and April 2002, Badger withheld $76,985 from employee paychecks for the payment of

healthcare premiums, including the amount specified in Count 1. During the same period Badger actually paid over $140,000 in medical claims, as well as $71,000 in MBA administration fees and stop-loss insurance premiums. Thus, in total, Badger paid over $211,000 in expenses related to health insurance during that ten-month period, almost three times the $76,985 Badger withheld from employees for health-care during that time; even considering claims only, Badger paid out almost twice as much as it deducted.[87]

As to counts 5–9, Bertocchi argued that "the government offered no evidence that Whiting or Badger misused, or even used, the employee 401(k) contributions. To the contrary, Badger's controller testified that while Badger continued to deduct the 401(k) money from employee paychecks throughout the charged period, the funds 'remained in the operating account of Badger' until LaSalle foreclosed on its assets."[88]

The next issue Bertocchi brought to the attention of the appeals court was the abuse of the so-called "wealth evidence" that the government misused during trial. The "wealth evidence," which involved my compensation and personal assets, was evidence that my trial attorney had argued to the court was irrelevant to the charges in the indictment. The government had countered that it needed this evidence admitted to prove willful-ness and intent to defraud on the conversion counts. During my appeal, Bertocchi argued that "the government did not stick to its theory: it made a bare pass at using the evidence to establish willfulness and not attempt to link it to intent to defraud. Instead, the government used Whiting's 'wealth' to induce class bias. The jury was thus left with all unfair prejudice and no relevance."[89]

And the last issue involved the district court having improperly adding the more than $850,000 in unpaid medical claims to increase my sentence and restitution. As we argued to the appellate court, the district court had wrongfully reasoned that the two false statement counts (counts 10 and 13) somehow caused the unpaid healthcare claims not to be paid.[90]

A Partial Victory

In September 2006, Bertocchi and Giampietro made their respective arguments to a three-judge panel at the Seventh Circuit Court in Chicago. Three months later, on December 15, 2006, the appellate court rendered its decision. They agreed with our argument that the district court had abused its discretion when it used the more than $850,000 in unpaid healthcare claims to increase my sentence and restitution, but it denied my other claims. As such, my case was sent back to the district court for resentencing.

I thought that under the circumstances, my attorney Joel Bertocchi did an excellent job. There were perhaps many more issues to raise before the appeals court, but rules of that court limit the size of the appeal document in terms of word count, which in turn limits our issues. In any event, I really thought the appeals court would see that this case had been one of bad prosecution all around and would throw out the entire case, but they didn't and I was starting to come to the realization that given how our criminal justice system works this was not going to go away anytime soon, if at all.

Chapter 15

A Reprieve

A S A RESULT OF WINNING PART OF MY APPEAL, the Seventh
Circuit Court sent a mandate requiring the district court to
resentence me without using unpaid health claims as part of the
picture. The question was would the government or the court
find some other creative way to sentence me to the same ninety-
month term or would they finally do the right thing and reduce
my sentence.

Hiring a New Attorney

I had to hire a new attorney experienced in federal sentencing since I had no intention of hiring Fitzgerald for the resentencing. I found a local attorney in Milwaukee named Jeremy
Levinson who was experienced in employment law and came
well-recommended.

During my first meeting with Levinson, in August 2007 up
at the prison camp in Duluth, we discussed the unpaid healthcare claims at Badger as well as those of Dale Garber at Western
Rubber. At the time, I was still in a court battle over the unpaid
healthcare claims at Badger with the union. Levinson strongly

recommended that I settle this lawsuit with the union before going before Judge Randa for resentencing. Doing so would give me a much better chance of reducing my sentence and show the court that I had taken care of these claims even though I was not required to under the law. I agreed and instructed my civil attorney, Bob Chapman, to negotiate a settlement. A few weeks later, the parties agreed on an amount of approximately $150,000, and the lawsuit was dismissed.

Levinson also thought that I should attempt to resolve the Dale Garber healthcare claims that Judge Randa had initially added to my restitution. I also agreed with this approach. Chapman contacted the Western union's attorney who in turn contacted Dale Garber. Garber had filed a claim with the U.S. Probations Office stating that Western had failed to pay $356,000 of his claims. I instructed my attorney to offer Garber $5,000 in full settlement, and he agreed to it, much to my surprise. Perhaps, I thought, the medical providers he owed had written the entire amount off and he would just keep the $5,000 for himself. Instead, as I found out later, Garber had not even been working at Western nor was he insured during the time he incurred the $356,000 in health claims that he and the government claimed was Western's and my responsibility.

After Giampietro found out about this proposed $5,000 settlement with Garber, he told Levinson that this amount would not be sufficient, so, as it turned out, this settlement was never completed. Nevertheless, the settlement with Badger's union was concluded, and Levinson and I were prepared to go forward with the resentencing hearing before Judge Randa.

Shortly after hiring my new attorney, Levinson met with Giampietro along with my appellate attorney, Bertocchi. Due to the reduction in healthcare claims ordered by the appellate court, my new sentencing guidelines calculation was in the range of twenty-seven to thirty-three months. However, Giampietro insisted that he would argue that I deserved a fifty-four-month sentence based on what he thought was appropriate and attempted to get my attorney to agree to this sentence. We, on the other hand, were attempting to get Giampietro to agree to no more than thirty-three months. My attorneys met with Giampietro in an attempt to come to an agreed-upon sentence to jointly recommend to the court, but nothing was settled. It seemed to me that Giampietro was just playing games and was not going to budge from the fifty-four months he wanted.

Altered Evidence

It goes without saying that Giampietro must have been very unhappy about the appellate court's decision to overturn his attempt to increase my sentence and have the unpaid healthcare claims added to my restitution. I had already witnessed to what extent he was willing to go, legal or otherwise, in his pursuit and I assumed that now he would be capable of almost anything. Federal prosecutors don't like to lose.

Just as he had argued a frivolous obstruction-of-justice motion during my initial sentencing, which he lost, Giampietro used this resentencing opportunity to again claim that I somehow misled the Probation Office as to my assets and liabilities. This time around he became even more cunning so as to be sure to win. As the evidence strongly suggests, Giampietro took my original financial disclosure report, with exhibits—which he had received from the Probation Office—actually altered it, and then used this altered copy as an exhibit to his resentencing brief to argue his point.

Specifically, Giampietro claimed that my checking account balance was incorrect because the account balance in the checking account the day I signed my financial disclosure statement (July 6, 2005) and the amount I listed as a checking account balance in my financial disclosure statement were different. Well, they should be different due to the fact that checks had already been written against the checking account balance but had not yet cleared the bank. As such, the proper method was to list my checkbook balance on the day I signed the financial disclosure statement. In other words, showing a checking account "bank" balance on my financial disclosure statement, when checks had already been written against those funds, would certainly have been misleading.

Nevertheless, Giampietro goes on the argue, "[e]ven if Whiting were to argue that his answer was technically correct because the check was written—and the account obligated . . . , the resulting increase in equity in his Florida residence is not also reflected in Section G of his New Worth Statement."[91]

However, Giampietro was wrong. The mortgage balance on my residence as indicated in my financial disclosure form as of July 6, 2005 was correct, and a copy of the mortgage statement was attached as an exhibit to prove it.

So where is the evidence that shows Giampietro altered my original financial disclosure statement and used this altered document to support his argument that I misled the Probation Office? It's simple, when you compare my financial disclosure report on file with the Probation Office against the alleged copy of my report attached to "The United States of America's Re-Sentencing Memorandum," you will find that my mortgage statement supporting the mortgage balance indicated in my report is not there. Of course, Giampietro could not have made this argument that I misled the Probation Office if my mortgage statement had been attached.

Harassment and Bullying

It was my choice whether to accept Giampietro's fifty-four-month sentence recommendation or take my chances of a higher or lower sentence in court. Since I don't make deals with the devil, I decided not to. However, after Levinson made it clear to Giampietro that I would not agree to his fifty-four-month sentence, Giampietro then proceeded to threaten my wife with a federal indictment!

Giampietro claimed through his continuing investigation of my finances that he had discovered that Marie had allegedly made a material mis-statement on a mortgage application she had completed a few years earlier. In particular, he alleged that she had deliberately mis-stated her income and the length of time employed on this mortgage application. As I inspected this mortgage application, I found all of the information to be completely accurate. Besides, this mortgage was not in default and all payments have been made in a timely fashion.

I was aware from my research that this tactic of threatening innocent family members was routinely used by federal prosecutors to motivate defendants to plead out rather than go to trial. However, this approach was used in the early stages of a case, before trial, to help motivate a defendant to plead guilty. I never heard it being used by a federal prosecutor before a resentencing. I am sure that there are instances when a family member is truly involved in the crime of the defendants or knowingly received money involved in the crime. However, these tactics have been used plenty of times against innocent family members to force guilty pleas to secure a "win" for the prosecutor.

In any event, I refused to succumb to Giampietro's threats. Marie and I were willing to go to trial if by chance she was indicted and vigorously fight to prove his allegations were false and to make the case that this prosecutor was attempting to coerce me into accepting an unfair sentence. As it turned out, when he finally realized that I would not agree, he dropped the issue of indicting Marie.

Resentencing Hearing

On May 18, 2008, almost ten months after my appeal decision, my resentencing day arrived. I was able to participate from the prison via Internet using a closed-circuit TV. Both of my attorneys, Levinson and Bertocchi, were present in court.

The first matter taken up by the court was the issue of the obstruction-of-justice enhancement. After hearing arguments from both of my attorneys and from Giampietro, Judge Randa spoke. He said he agreed with the government that I had obstructed justice by misleading the court as to my assets and liabilities. I could not believe it but was by now pretty used to this type of sham justice. The result of this win by the government was that two more points were added to my "offense level" (the accumulation of points which determines the recommended incarceration pursuant to the federal sentencing guidelines), bringing it to twenty points, which called for a monthly sentencing range of thirty-three to forty-one months.

The judge then asked me if I wanted to speak. Levinson and I had spent a lot of time preparing my speech. I explained to the court that I regretted that the employee healthcare claims were not paid and if I could go back in time I would do things differently. Notwithstanding the fact that I had not done anything wrong and certainly nothing criminal, I was attempting to convey to the court that I regretted what had happened. The court acknowledged the fact that I had resolved the underfunded health claims matter with the Badger union even though I was not obliged to do so.

Then Judge Randa pronounced my new sentence: forty months of incarceration, down from the previous ninety months, and the same three years of supervised release. At least I fared better than I would have if I had taken Giampetro's offer of fifty-four months. Up to that point, even though I was innocent, this was a major win since very few individuals ever win anything in an appeal of their conviction let alone get their sentence reduced by over fifty percent. Nevertheless, I was still disappointed over the frivolous obstruction enhancement that Giampietro was able to push through, which ended up resulting in eight additional months for me in prison.

Home Again

Having already served twenty-five months, I was released from the Duluth Prison Camp just six months later, on the morning of November 24, 2008. Actually, most convicted defendants don't serve their entire sentences in prison. They typically get about forty-seven days off for every one year of the sentence imposed for good behavior. In addition, the last few months of the sentence can be spent in the halfway house. So I actually spent about thirty months in Duluth.

I was required to report to the halfway house located in Milwaukee by 1:00 P.M. the day of my release. Marie picked me up at the same administration building in which she had dropped me off two and a half years earlier. I arrived at the halfway house a little early to check in and was assigned a room to share with three other guys. I heard that many years earlier this halfway house had been used by priests as their living quarters since it was right next door to a church. The halfway house in Milwaukee—a three-story building with many rooms—was located in the inner city in a residential area run by the BOP. But even though I was released from prison, I was still in the custody of the BOP. Over the course of the next few weeks, I was able to go home but had to personally stop by the halfway house once a week to check in.

On March 24, 2009, I was formally released from the halfway house and BOP's custody to start my three years of supervised release. I met with my probation officer, who informed me about the requirements of supervised release. I quickly learned that I would meet with her each month and be required to fill out and submit a monthly report. I was not permitted to travel outside the district unless I received a written pre-approval and would be unable to continue my career as a business owner or consultant working for myself as I had done for the past thirty years since I was restricted from maintaining any fiduciary capacity during my supervised release. As I was informed by my probation officer, supervised release under the federal system was simply a continuation of the punishment.

Chapter 16

A Stand for Justice

AFTER HAVING GONE THROUGH, over the eight years prior to this writing, massive civil litigation, a federal indictment, a criminal trial, a sentencing, an appeal, a resentencing, over thirty months of incarceration, living in a halfway house, months of supervised release restrictions, and substantial negative press, I became more determined than ever to aggressively fight to clear my name and expose the real offenders in this case. Although my appeal could deal only with the events that had taken place at my trial and nothing more, my next legal challenge will be what is referred to as a collateral attack on my conviction. It will be in the form of a post-conviction motion in accordance with Federal Statute 28 U.S.C. § 2255 and will challenge my conviction based on my not receiving "effective assistance of counsel" at trial, resulting in my conviction.

Constitutional Violation

Effective assistance of counsel is something every citizen of this country is entitled to as guaranteed by the Constitution. Ineffective assistance of counsel is an issue raised in a post-conviction motion in criminal cases in which a defendant asserts that his criminal conviction occurred because his attorney failed to properly defend his case. This is a very high legal standard to meet and in order to prevail on such a claim, the defendant must show two things: (a) deficient performance by counsel (b) but for such deficiency, the result of the proceeding would have been different.

In the landmark court case *Strickland v. Washington*, the Supreme Court established the standard by which a counsel's performance should be judged in assessing whether it complies with the Constitution. If counsel "so undermined the proper functioning of the adversarial process that the trial cannot be relied upon as having produced a just result," then a claim of ineffectiveness will lie.[92]

Several problems result from ineffective assistance of counsel. First, ineffective assistance produces unjust convictions. Second, it creates a disparity in the adversarial process that substantially increases the chances of governmental abuse of power and undermines fundamental constitutional rights. Third, it stands in the way of reaching the goal of equal justice.

In my case, my defense attorney, Michael Fitzgerald, failed to properly investigate my case, resulting in his inability to develop an appropriate trial strategy to challenge the government's case, and as such "undermined the proper functioning of the adversarial process," which our criminal justice system relies on in producing "a just result."[93] Consequently, my constitutional right under the Sixth Amendment of the Constitution to effective assistance of trial counsel was violated. I deserve and thus am demanding a new trial.

Evidence in my case shows that Fitzgerald substantially failed to investigate my case and properly prepare for trial. His failure to investigate and present crucial exculpatory evidence to the jury was not based on any "reasonable litigation strategy" but rather was due to a failure to investigate, lack of trial preparation, unprofessional judgments, and flawed views of legal principles. As a result of Fitzgerald's ineffectiveness, key exculpatory evidence demonstrating my innocence was not presented to the jury and witnesses were not effectively impeached. As such, the jury in this case actually received only half the story—the government's story. During trial, I was acquitted on counts 2, 11, and 12. However, the following evidence—which my defense attorney failed to investigate and present to the jury—demonstrates my innocence on all counts for which I was convicted.

Count 1

I was charged and convicted of allegedly misusing $6,134 of funds intended for the payment of the June 2001 health insurance premiums that had been deducted from the paychecks of Badger Die Casting employees. However, my defense counsel failed to investigate the following:

- On June 4, 2001, Badger paid $41,068.16 to United Healthcare, which included employees' June 2001 contributions of $6,134. Furthermore, in June 2001, all Badger employees had been covered by United, resulting in all their June 2001 claims being paid for by United.[94]

- From the time I purchased Badger in July 1998 through the time Badger was taken over by Randy Lubben in April 2002, Badger paid out almost $1.2 million in health insurance premiums but collected only about $178,000 in employee healthcare contributions. That means Badger paid out over $1 million more from its own pocket than it collected from Badger employees.[95]

- During the same month that the government claims I had, in essence, stolen over $6,000 of employees' funds, I provided Badger with $65,000 of my own cash to help meet one of its payroll. This money was never repaid to me.[96]

Counts 3 and 4

I was charged and convicted of allegedly converting almost $40,000 of funds intended for the payment of the June 2001 through February 2002 health insurance premiums which had been deducted from the paychecks of Western Rubber employees. However, defense counsel failed to investigate the following:

- From April 1, 2001, through February 28, 2002, Western collected a little over $59,000 in employee payroll deductions and paid out a little over $100,000 in healthcare costs—paying out almost $42,000 more than what was collected from employees.[97]

- From June 2001 through February 2002, I received a little over $63,000 from Western in payment of compensation and building rent. However, I paid out a little over $86,000 for Western's building mortgage payments, which included a $50,000 personal loan to Western. That meant I paid out some $22,000 more in funds then I had received from Western.[98]

Counts 5–9

I was charged and convicted of allegedly converting $20,000 of funds intended for the payment of the January through May 2002 401(k), plan which had been deducted from the paychecks of Badger Die Casting employees. Bussan, as a key government witness, falsely testified at trial that Badger employees' 401(k) contributions, totaling just over $20,000, remained in Badger's checking account and as such were used to pay Badger's expenses. However, evidence not presented at trial shows that when Bussan failed to pay over Badger employees' 401(k) contributions, these contributions were in fact never left in Badger's checking account to be used for something else but rather remained in Badger's assets until they were paid. Badger's assets were then transferred by LaSalle Bank to Randy Lubben's company, WDC, and WDC failed to pay over these employee 401(k) contributions to Strong Funds.[99]

In late 2001, Bussan fell behind in providing payroll data to Strong. In early 2002, I learned of this problem and directed Bussan to send Strong the delinquent December 2001 401(k) contributions. Bussan prepared a check in an amount equal to the delinquent December 2001 contributions, but that check was not honored by LaSalle Bank, which after consultation with Bussan, chose to pay other bills with the funds available, without my knowledge or consent.

Subsequently, I instructed Bussan to wire the delinquent December 2001 contributions to Strong, and Bussan prepared that wire. However, the wire was not honored by LaSalle for the same reason, without my knowledge or consent. Nevertheless, Bussan informed me that the December 2001 401(k) contributions had been paid by wire transfer.

From January 2002 to April 2002, Bussan never provided Strong the payroll data needed to calculate the 401(k) plan contributions, interfering with both my and Strong's ability to determine what contributions might be due to the 401(k) plan. In fact, Bussan did not provide this payroll data to Strong until June 2002, by which time Badger had ceased operations when its assets were foreclosed upon by LaSalle and its business assumed by an unrelated entity, Wisconsin Die Castings (WDC), for whom Bussan immediately assumed the same position as controller.

It was Bussan, not I, who determined which checks would ultimately clear the bank. Funds necessary to pay the contributions were available to Bussan during these months, but Bussan, unbeknownst to me, never provided the payroll data to Strong and, as a result, the contributions were not made to Strong and the assets representing those contributions were diverted by LaSalle Bank to WDC.[100]

What is even more interesting is that, after my trial, I sued Bussan for his negligence in failing to pay over the Badger employees' 401(k) contributions. I won a judgment against Bussan, and he has since paid the judgment.[101]

Lubben's company, WDC, as a matter of law, was responsible for payment of Badger employees' 401(k) contributions. Federal case law in the Seventh Circuit Court, which covers the state of Wisconsin, mandates that a purchaser of a business is liable for unpaid pension liability if the purchaser had knowledge of the liability and acquired substantially most of the company's assets. According to Lubben's own deposition testimony, he had clear knowledge of Badger's 401(k) liability, purchased Badger's assets with such knowledge, and continued his business, WDC, with substantially the same Badger employees, same equipment, same customers, and at the same location. If jurors had been informed about this critical evidence, it is highly unlikely they would have convicted me.[102]

Evidence not provided to the jury shows that approximately $100,000 said to have been paid to me during the months of January and February 2002 for expense reimbursements, was in fact paid out to fund Badger's raw material purchases. Absent this key evidence, the government was able to argue to jurors that this

$100,000 was paid directly to me as an expense reimbursement during the same relevant time Badger employee 401(k) contributions were not being transmitted to Strong Funds.[103] In fact, these $100,000 in payments were made payable to my management company, Garrett Group, and exchanged at my bank for a cashier's check payable to Badger's raw material supplier, since Badger had to pay for their raw material purchases "cash on delivery." I never received any benefit from this $100,000 payment by Badger. But the government made it look as though I had.

Count 10

I was charged and convicted of knowingly and willfully making a material false statement when I allegedly caused a document to be disseminated at Badger Die Casting titled "Important Insurance Information Meeting Notice" that represented to employees that MBA had been selected as "our new health insurance carrier" knowing that such statement was materially false.

On May 17, 2005, Thresa Palkowski testified, as a key government witness, that I had instructed her to post a notice of Badger's change in health insurance plan from United Healthcare to MBA. It was undisputed at trial that the terms of the union contract permitted Badger to make such a change to a self-funded healthcare plan.

According to Palkowski's trial testimony, after she provided me with a draft of a notice, I directed her to insert the language "MBA as our new health insurance carrier" rather than the wording "MBA as our new administrator," which had been the wording she allegedly intended to use.[104] Palkowski further testified that after she made this change, she placed her name and the date at the bottom of the page and posted this notice to inform Badger employees of the health insurance change. Most notably, there was absolutely no evidence admitted at trial that any Badger employee relied on this notice or that any Badger employee thought the language "MBA as our new health insurance carrier" was false or misleading.[105]

Nevertheless, shortly after trial, Palkowski provided sworn testimony in a civil deposition that in fact she "c[ame] up with the language that was in the [meeting notice]"; she "d[idn't] recall at whose direction . . . t[he] line was added . . . [a]s our new health insurance carrier"; and, she did not remember "Whiting having *any role* in the selection of the language that's there in the [meeting notice]." Palkowski further testified the only time she provided Whiting with a copy of this meeting notice was after it was posted.[106]

About seven months later, my civil attorney Robert Chapman requested a meeting with Palkowski to discuss her recent recanted testimony. She told Chapman she did not want to meet because "she feared she would implicate herself."[107]

But there is more. In December 2008, I hired an investigator named Paul Ciolino to meet with Palkowski to discuss her involvement with Badger's health insurance plan. In a personal interview, Palkowski stated to Ciolino that it would have "been unlikely" that Whiting "picked the language" used in the meeting notice. She also stated that during her trial testimony, "she simply could not remember much of what she was being asked," and therefore "much of what she testified to in court could have been flawed." Palkowski further stated that she "did in fact misspeak 'on an occasion or two' . . . [and] was sure she did due to the way the questions were asked."[108]

Sadly, this new evidence portrays a witness deliberately lying while in the presence of government prosecutors—perhaps motivated by fear and intimidation—and then shortly after trial, testifying under oath to a completely different set of facts demonstrating my innocence. With that being said, although I personally believe that Palkowski innocently selected the language "MBA as our new health insurance carrier" and didn't intend to mislead anyone, she should have stood her ground rather than say what the government prosecutors wanted her to say to support their theory to the jury.

Count 13

I was charged and convicted of knowingly and willfully making a false statement and representation to Western Rubber's controller and general manager that I allegedly had a plan to provide for the cancer treatments of a Western employee, knowing that such statements were false. However, defense counsel failed to investigate the following:

- Garber was not entitled to any healthcare coverage during the time he incurred his medical bills because on or about May 31, 2001, he left his employment with Western and failed to pay any COBRA premium payments thereafter. In fact, the government told the jury that "[y]ou will hear testimony from Dale Garber that his medical bills exceed $250,000 and were never paid by Western Rubber at all."[109] As it turned out, Garber never did testify and the government never admitted evidence that Garber had any legitimate medical bills that were the responsibility of Western.[110]

- I had a plan to provide funding for Western employees' legitimate unpaid healthcare claims, including Garber's. Part of Western's business was sold to Viking Industries, and the remaining assets of Western were liquidated and paid to LaSalle Bank as senior lender. Since I was not involved in administering Western's payroll or in the collection of employee health insurance contributions, I was unaware of the legality of the government's allegations that Western was responsible for Garber's healthcare claims. After I was indicted and had reviewed all the allegations including the allegations in Count 13, I instructed my defense counsel to audit Western's healthcare plan to determine the legitimacy of the government's claims. I also provided evidence to my defense counsel that I did in fact have a plan to fund any legitimate unpaid healthcare claims, including Garber's, from the proceeds of Western's liquidation.[111]

- I informed Allen DeSomer, Western's controller, that I had a plan to provide funding for Garber's legitimate medical claims from the proceeds of the liquidation of Western assets. In fact, DeSomer's affidavit to that effect has been submitted to the court in my motion for a new trial.[112]

Criminal Intent

Intent is the key factor in determining whether a particular event is criminal or civil. Each one of the counts for which I was convicted required that the jury find that I had the prerequisite criminal intent—that I intentionally, knowingly, and deliberately committed the offense. Absent this showing, there is no crime.

Rarely in white-collar criminal cases, does the government show this criminal intent at trial through "direct evidence" such as the defendant admitting that he committed the offense with a "culpable mind." Instead, the law of our land permits the government to demonstrate criminal intent through what is called circumstantial evidence. My jury instructions defined circumstantial evidence as "the proof of a series of facts which tend to show whether the defendant is guilty or not guilty." It is kind of like putting enough dots on a piece of paper, each dot signifying a fact or an event, and then the government explains why all the dots should be connected together thereby signifying criminal intent.

In my case, the government's strategy was to show jurors through circumstantial evidence that the reason I committed these criminal offenses was due to my "systematic draining of funds from the companies—through exorbitant management fees and expenses—to support his lavish lifestyle [which] put the companies in a situation where the defendant was prompted to, and did, convert the employee funds that are charged."[113]

As the government argued to the court in its successful attempt to use the evidence of my income and personal assets during trial "the theory of the government's case is . . . the defendant withdrew significant amounts of money in management fees and other related expenses. And with those funds, used them to purchase significant assets, such that by the time 2001 rolled around, there was . . . insufficient funds in these businesses with which to honor his obligations, which are the subject of the indictment . . . It goes to the issue of motive and intent."[114]

In other words, according to the government, my "criminal intent" was displayed by taking unjustified and significant compensation from Badger and Western for the purpose of using my compensation to purchase significant assets, which in turn caused "insufficient funds in these businesses with which to honor obligations, which are the subject of the indictment." Even though my defense attorney adamantly objected, the government was permitted by the court to use my compensation and personal assets based on their representations as to the use of this evidence.

The government proceeded to tell jurors during opening statements at trial: "[t]he evidence will show that the defendant acquired Badger Die and Western Rubber . . . [and] began withdrawing significant management fees . . . [and] used his management fees to fund the purchase of significant assets for . . . himself. Among some of those things were . . . a $700,000 condo in Florida, a $1.3 million home in Brookfield, and a $145,000 R.V."[115]

However, as you will see, government prosecutors are master illusionists: using smoke and mirrors during their trial performance, they convinced their audience (the jury) to believe something happened (a crime)—when in fact it didn't. This government duplicity that went unchallenged by a defense attorney who failed to properly investigate my case had a devastating result for an innocent defendant: conviction and extensive incarceration.

During my trial, the government argued that I had allegedly pocketed $2.6 million in compensation from Badger and Western during the period of my ownership. However, my defense attorney failed to audit Badger's and Western's books to determine just what my real compensation was. In fact, the evidence they failed to investigate or present to the jury demonstrates that I used most of that amount paid to me to provide Badger and Western with operating capital and loans and in payment of their direct expenses.

The result was that during the period in which I owned Badger, my actual annual average compensation was just over $110,000 as CEO and president. In comparison, Randy Lubben, Badger's vice president of sales and marketing, was compensated $110,000 a year, and the previous owners of Badger, the Strassmans, were paid approximately $120,000 per year each. During the period that I owned Western, my actual annual average compensation was just over $170,000 as Western's CEO and president. In comparison, other CEOs and presidents working in the same area, at companies of similar size, had an average annual compensation of $279,214.[116] Clearly, if this evidence had been presented to the jury, it would have demonstrated that my compensation was well under the market and did not show that I was "draining" or "looting" my companies.

Next, the government argued that I had absolutely no risk during my ownership of Badger and Western. However, evidence my attorney failed to investigate shows that I had over $10 million in personal financial risk in owning Badger and Western.[117] Then, the government argued to the jury that my compensation led to the closing of both Badger and Western, which consequently caused employee healthcare benefits to not be paid. "He took all the money he could out of them, and to the point where he had to start taking money from his employees . . . he took so much that both the companies ultimately folded."[118] However, as I have presented in my motion for a new trial, Badger's and Western's cash-flow problems had nothing to do with my compensation but rather with operating losses.[119]

Besides all of this, the government never provided any evidence at trial that any of my compensation from Badger and Western was used to purchase any of my personal assets. Consequently, had Fitzgerald properly done his job, he could have easily dismantled the government case against me leading the jury to conclude that I had absolutely no "criminal intent."

And lastly, during the relevant time (2001 to 2002) in which the government alleged that I needed to misuse $66,117 of employee payroll deductions, my four companies produced over $41 million in sales; paid out over $15 million in employee wages, payroll taxes, and benefits; and had $20 million in collective company assets. In addition, I maintained an employee 401(k) fund with over $2 million in total assets. Had my defense counsel investigated the sheer size of my organization relative to the amount alleged converted and presented such evidence during my trial, jurors would have quickly realized how ridiculous and outrageous the government's allegations really were and what a complete waste had been made of perhaps well over a million dollars of taxpayer money in the prosecution of this case against me.[120]

Filing My Motion

All of these issues have been included in my brief titled "Motion Under 28 U.S.C. § 2255 to Vacate, Set Aside, or Correct Sentence By a Person in Federal Custody," which was filed with the U.S. District Court Eastern District of Wisconsin on July 27, 2009.[121] Since I had spent close to three thousand hours in the prison law library and several months researching the issues applicable to this legal proceeding once I was released from prison, I decided to draft and file this motion myself. My motion requests that the court vacate my conviction and dismiss the charges against me with prejudice or alternatively vacate my conviction and order a new trial under the conditions that guarantee my constitutional rights.

My motion also included a two-hundred-page exhibit that incorporated evidence that supports the claims in my motion. A few days later, I filed with the court a forensic accounting report, prepared by Dennis Czurylo, which verified all of the financial data in my exhibit.[122]

Government's Response

After taking almost a year to respond, AUSA Gimapietro, as expected, did his best to attack my motion from a legal perspective and joined forces with my trial lawyer, Michael Fitzgerald, who included an affidavit that attempted to combat my motion on the merits.[123] Right or wrong, no defense attorney ever wants to be found "ineffective" by a court.

The crux of the government's response in opposition to my motion to vacate my conviction was that whatever Fitzgerald did or neglected to do in preparing for my trial and his trial conduct was "reasonable litigation strategy."[124] Most notably, as he admitted in his affidavit, his entire trial strategy was limited to "cross-examination of government witnesses,"[125] since, according to Fitzgerald, Badger's and Western's records were "turned over to Mr. Whiting and were in his custody and control";[126] "Mr. Whiting adamantly refused to testify in his own defense";[127] and, "the potential harm from the government's cross-examination of Mr. Ruffin outweighed the potential benefit of this testimony."[128] In my opinion, these were all excuses for his unprofessional conduct and were disingenuous.

My Reply Brief

I filed my reply brief to the government's response in May 2010.[129] I addressed what I deemed to be frivolous legal arguments by the government and responded to Fitzgerald's list of excuses for his deficiencies before and during trial including presenting evidence demonstrating that he was not truthful in his affidavit. I summed up my reply brief to the court as follows:

> As the government acknowledges, under the applicable legal standard, this Court need not decide whether Whiting would have or should have been acquitted or if a crime was actually committed, only that

there is *at least* a "reasonable probability" that but for counsel's unprofessional errors, the result of the trial would have been different. As such, Whiting submits that there is a "reasonable probability" that the result of his trial would have been different had the jury learned:

- Badger paid employees' June 2001 healthcare contributions toward United Healthcare's June 2001 premium;

- Whiting provided Badger $55,000 more in cash than he received from Badger in June 2001;

- Western paid employees' June 2001 to February 2002 healthcare contributions toward healthcare plan premiums, benefits, and administration costs;

- Whiting paid out $22,278.97 more in cash from June 2001 to February 2002 then he received in return from Western;

- Bussan informed Whiting he had wired the December 2001 401(k) contributions to Strong;

- Employee 401(k) contributions were never left in Badger's bank accounts and thus were never "used";

- Bussan, not Whiting, was the "fiduciary" as it relates to transmitting employees' 401(K) contributions to Strong;

- Wisconsin Die Casting, as a matter of law, was liable for Badger's underfunded 401(k) contributions;

- Dall was not qualified to provide expert testimony that Wisconsin Die Casting was not liable for Badger's 401(k) contributions;

- Whiting did not receive approximately $100,000 in alleged reimbursements from Badger;

- Dale Garber was not entitled to health insurance benefits after May 31, 2001;

- Whiting had a plan to fund Garber's healthcare benefits had he been eligible to receive such benefits;

- Whiting's compensation as Badger's and Western's CEO and President was not $2.6 million;

- Whiting had almost $10 million in personal financial risk during his ownership of Badger and Western;

- Badger's and Western's cash-flow problems were directly related to operating losses, not Whiting's compensation.

Unfortunately, this case exemplifies what can happen to a defendant with overzealous prosecutors and a defense attorney who fails to provide constitutionally effective assistance of counsel, the result of which is an unfair trial. In light of these numerous and substantial unprofessional errors, there can be no "confidence" that the outcome of Whiting's trial would have been the same. (*Strickland v. Washington*, 466 U.S. 668, 694 (1984)). Both alone and together, these unprofessional errors denied Whiting a fair trial in which the government's case was vigorously tested by the adversarial process, which is the bedrock of our legal system.[130]

Justice Is Still Waiting

In light of the numerous cases over the past few years whereby innocent citizens have been victimized and convicted of crimes at the hands of prosecutors, a new ethics rule has been passed and enacted in an effort to help curb and remedy this pervasive problem. In particular, this rule requires that "[w]hen a prosecutor knows of new, credible and material evidence creating a reasonable likelihood that a convicted defendant did not commit an offense of which the defendant was convicted, the prosecutor shall . . . (ii) undertake further investigation, or make a reasonable effort to cause an investigation, to determine whether the defendant was convicted of an offense that the defendant did not commit."[131]

Nevertheless, AUSA Giampietro refuses to conduct *any* such investigation of the extensive exculpatory evidence presented in my 2255 motion. Instead, he continues to spend taxpayer money in his personal effort to defeat my pursuit of justice and to protect his conviction and perhaps his career.

Part Two

A SERIOUSLY FLAWED JUDICIAL SYSTEM

Chapter 17

Overview of the Federal Criminal Justice System

IF YOU HAVE NOT YET come to the startling conclusion that the only thing that stands in the way of most business people doing serious time in a federal penitentiary is the choice by prosecutors as to whom they will target, you will by the time you finish reading this book. Today, entrepreneurs and business owners face enough uncertainty in the current economic climate without having to be concerned about the chance of going to prison because a determined federal prosecutor can persuade a jury that they violated a vague and ambiguous federal law.

The U.S. economy is resilient, but if the current onslaught of federal prosecution of white-collar crimes continues, a vigorous economic recovery is perhaps less likely. This is a very serious problem in our country which continues to take place each and every day with no end in sight. But this all starts with understanding how the unfortunate among us get ensnared by the federal criminal justice system.

Government's Criminal Investigators

The responsibility to investigate and prosecute federal crimes in the United States rests with the executive branch of government through the Department of Justice (DOJ). All federal prosecutors are part of the DOJ. However, there are many other federal agencies that refer criminal cases to the DOJ. Although the Federal Bureau of Investigation (FBI) is the principal investigative arm of the DOJ, agents of the U.S. Postal Inspection Services (U.S. postal inspectors) are authorized to investigate criminal activity that utilizes or affects the U.S. mail system. The Drug Enforcement Administration (DEA) is authorized to investigate violations such as drug trafficking and possession of controlled substances with the intent to distribute, and the Bureau of Alcohol, Tobacco and Firearms (ATF) investigates illegal fire arms possession, sales, and transfers. Other more notable federal agencies include:

- Environmental Protection Agency (EPA)

- U.S. Secret Service (USSS)

- Internal Revenue Service (IRS)

- Department of Labor (DOL)

- Department of Transportation (DOT)

- Federal Trade Commission (FTC)

- Securities and Exchange Commission (SEC)

- U.S. Immigration and Custom Enforcement (ICE)

- Department of Interior

- Department of Agriculture

These federal agencies have special agents who are all too eager to start a criminal investigation on some unsuspecting businessperson. The personal motivation of these special agents perhaps are many when it comes to deciding if a case should go down the path of criminal or civil. But clearly, high-profile criminal cases like the Martha Stewart prosecution place these special agents in the limelight, which undoubtedly helps their careers. Another incentive for the agent is that overseeing criminal cases might help him or her pursue a career such as becoming an investigator with the FBI.

Even aside from the personal goals of these special agents, federal agencies must investigate and refer a certain number of criminal cases to demonstrate to Congress their oversight capabilities. This, I fear, places many cases that would otherwise be civil in nature into criminal territory.

Since these governmental agencies don't have the ability to initiate and prosecute alleged crimes on their own, they need to contact the U.S. Attorney's Office in the district where the crime allegedly took place and attempt to "sell" their case to that office's prosecutor.

Basic Structure

Just like each state, the federal government has its own criminal statutes, court system, prosecutors, and investigative and police agencies with authority to investigate and prosecute criminal offenses. Crimes most frequently prosecuted by the federal government involve drug trafficking, organized crime, and financial and fraud crimes, whereas the states mainly prosecute crimes against individuals, such as murders, assaults, robberies, thefts, and crimes against property. States can only prosecute crimes committed within their respective boundaries. The federal government can prosecute crimes anywhere within the United States.

The executive branch of the federal government is responsible for investigating and prosecuting all federal crimes. All federal prosecutors, investigators, and policing officers are members of the executive branch of government. Furthermore, all federal prosecutors, including the investigating officers of the FBI, DEA, and ATF, including U.S. marshals, are employed by the DOJ, which is under the direction of the attorney general appointed by the president. There are ninety-three U.S. attorneys who prosecute cases in their respective districts. Each of these ninety-three U.S. attorneys appoints assistant U.S. attorneys to help prosecute criminal cases.

With regard to the federal judiciary, there are three levels of federal courts and federal judges to hear criminal cases.

The first level is comprised of ninety-four U.S. federal courts, presided over by U.S. district court judges and U.S. magistrate judges. All federal criminal trials take place in the U.S. district courts.

The next level is made up of the thirteen U.S. courts of appeals, which have jurisdiction over particular geographic areas called circuits. Each appellate court hears appeals from the district courts within their respective circuits. For example, the Seventh Circuit Court of Appeals that heard my appeal has jurisdiction over the U.S. District Court in the Eastern District of Wisconsin where my trial took place. A person convicted of a federal crime has a legal right to appeal to the appellate court having jurisdiction.

The third and highest level is the Supreme Court, which is composed of nine judges. The Supreme Court acts as an appellate court reviewing the decisions of the thirteen U.S. courts of appeals. In a federal criminal case, there is generally no legal right to appeal to the Supreme Court; however, the person seeking review can file an application (called a petition for a writ of certiorari) for review by this court. If the applicant is fortunate enough to have his or her case heard by the Supreme Court, this court's decision is final and not subject to further appeal.

How One Is Charged With a Federal Crime

When an investigating agent from one of the many federal agencies believes there is evidence of a violation of U.S. criminal law, he or she presents these findings to the office of the U.S. attorney in his or her district. An assistant U.S. attorney (AUSA) will review the case and question the agent about the findings to determine if there is sufficient evidence to show probable cause that a federal crime has been committed. The simple definition of probable cause is a reasonable belief that a person has committed a crime. If the AUSA determines that there is probable cause, he or she will present evidence to the grand jury and ask it to vote on the proposed criminal charges drafted by the AUSA. (I will discuss the grand jury system in chapter 18.)

If, on the other hand, evidence is insufficient to establish probable cause, then the case could take one of two directions: the AUSA may present the case to the grand jury and have the grand jury continue the investigation; or the AUSA may ask the agent to continue the investigation on his own. In certain situations, when there is not enough time to present the case to the grand jury, the AUSA will file a complaint with the district court setting forth the facts and offenses charged and ask the judge to issue an arrest warrant. However, after the defendant is arrested, the AUSA still must present the case to the grand jury and obtain an indictment.

The Adversarial System

According to Wikipedia.com, the definition of adversarial system is "a legal system where two advocates represent their parties' positions before an impartial person or group of people, usually a jury or judge, who attempt to determine the truth of the case." But, our federal criminal justice system is much more adversarial and antagonistic then this simple definition implies.

In a perfect world, the adversarial system puts in opposition two equally competent, resourceful, dedicated, and intelligent advocates against one another. An impartial judge presides over the tribunal providing the law for the unbiased fact-finder, be it a judge or jury, who evaluates the evidence against the law.

In theory, this just and open proceeding creates an environment for the truth to materialize. In other words, the adversarial system is supposed to maximize the likelihood that all relevant facts and arguments will be placed before the judge or jury so that the truth can be determined. But this is just not how it works in the real world.

The key advocates in the federal justice system are the prosecutor, who represents the federal government, and the defense attorney, who represents the accused. While good and ethical defense attorneys will of course do their absolute best for their clients even in light of the fact that they lose most of their cases that go to trial, the prosecutor's culture places winning above all else.

Failure to win a case is injurious to a prosecutor's career path since it appears to show lack of skill and/or poor professional judgment in obtaining an indictment that is later dismissed. A prosecutor's career is enhanced by being known as a "winner," which enables him or her to get more visible cases and obtain a higher position and compensation in the prosecutor's office. Also, as we have seen, the career path of a successful prosecutor can lead to a position in the White House, a judgeship in the district or appellate courts, or a position as the attorney general. Many times for federal prosecutors, the temptation to cut corners rather than do the right thing is just too great.

This tends to stack the deck against the defense attorney and of course the innocent defendant. And the unscrupulous prosecutor who is willing to win at all costs can begin to implement his tactics well before the defendant has even been indicted.

Federal prosecutors have complete discretion as to whether to charge an individual with a crime or not. Prosecutors also have complete discretion in determining what charges to seek, and in some instances they can even interpret the law so that it suits their needs in a particular case. Congress drafts criminal laws very broadly with the intention of allowing federal courts to largely define what conduct they deem criminal. But when a prosecutor decides to interpret the language of federal criminal statutes to cover certain conduct under investigation, with the court concurring, this can lead to an expansion of criminal laws well outside what Congress intended. (I will discuss this in more detail in the section titled "Overcriminalization.")

And finally, due to the sheer number and depth of our federal criminal laws, prosecutors can charge an individual with several crimes all based on the same underlying conduct. In fact, this tactic of "overcharging" by prosecutors is quite common in the federal system. By filing as many charges as possible, the prosecutor substantially improves his chances of winning a conviction should the evidence on many of the counts be insufficient to win over a jury. Overcharging is also used in plea bargaining by the prosecutor since he can agree to drop most of the charges in return for a guilty plea by the defendant. (I will discuss overcharging in greater detail later.)

Federal prosecutors have many more advantages over the defense. During the investigation phase of a case, prosecutors will generally secure cooperation by obtaining indictments on others they believe participated in the alleged criminal conduct. Prosecutors will then obtain plea agreements from those defendants who, as a condition, are required to cooperate as government witnesses in helping the government secure indictments against others. Prosecutors will also intimidate other individuals whom they intend not to charge into testifying favorably for the government.

The less-than-scrupulous prosecutor knows how to use the system to win convictions against the innocent in the following ways: misusing evidence, misleading the court, making unsupported arguments to jury, suborning perjury, and withholding exculpatory evidence from the defense. We will look at each of these things later in the book.

Chapter 18

The Federal Grand Jury System

A GRAND JURY CONSISTS OF between sixteen and twenty-three citizens who have the obligation, after reviewing the evidence, to vote on a criminal charge presented by the prosecutor. Generally, the grand jury hears only evidence presented by the government—*nothing from the defense.* In order for a person to be indicted, at least twelve members of the grand jury must find that there is probable cause to believe that the person who is the subject of the proceeding committed a crime. The grand jury does not determine whether the defendant is guilty or innocent—that is determined at trial.

The Fifth Amendment to the U.S. Constitution requires that charges for all capital and "infamous" crimes be brought by an indictment returned by a grand jury. The Supreme Court has held that an "infamous" crime is one that is punished by imprisonment for over one year.[132]

In addition, individuals accused of a federal crime punishable by more than one year of incarceration have a constitutional right to be indicted by a grand jury.

The federal grand jury process was initially intended to protect citizens from overzealous government prosecutions. However, it has been turned into a manipulative system whereby prosecutors can secure indictments on just about anyone who unluckily ends up in their crosshairs. Federal prosecutors routinely misuse the grand jury process. Grand jury witnesses are not allowed to be represented by an attorney. As such, prosecutors can use the proceeding to shape and coerce their witnesses' testimony. This secret testimony can later be used by prosecutors during trial to keep their witnesses in line as they, in most all cases, win their conviction. In addition, despite the fact that this practice is prohibited by the "DOJ U.S. Attorney Manual," I believe prosecutors often use the grand jury as an instrument for pre-trial discovery of evidence to assist in their trial strategy.

History of Grand Juries

Today, grand juries are virtually unknown outside the United States. Most countries have abolished them, replacing them with the preliminary hearing, a procedure by which a judge hears evidence concerning the alleged offenses and makes a decision as to whether the prosecution can proceed. This method is better for defendants since the prosecutor is usually required to persuade the judge in a public hearing that it has sufficient evidence to secure a conviction. Also, the defendant can see the evidence and cross-examine the prosecution witnesses. This can weed out any behind-closed-door shenanigans being perpetrated by the prosecutor.

The concept of the grand jury began in England. During the years 980 through 1016, under the law of Anglo-Saxon King Aethelred, twelve landowners would be appointed to investigate alleged crimes. Then, starting in the year 1166, Henry II would send out a group of twelve men sworn to report all crimes committed since the last session of the circuit court. Later, the notion of a grand jury was recognized by King John in the Magna Carta signed in 1215 where it established various procedures to ensure fairness in the administration of justice.

Until the mid-1300s, twelve-man juries served to present indictments and rule on the legitimacy of charges. From 1312 to 1377, during Edward III's reign, the twelve-man juries were replaced with twenty-four knights chosen by the county sheriff, who had authority for starting the prosecution. This group of knights was called the "le grand inquest." The twelve men, having lost their original inquisitorial jurisdiction, became known as the petit jury, which had the responsibility for deciding the guilt or innocence of individuals in capital crimes. By the fourteenth century, this common law relating to criminal proceedings resulted in two prominent procedural policies: an indicting grand jury and an adjudicating petit jury.

In 1642, the English legal philosopher, Edward Coke, interpreted certain Magna Carta provisions as preserving life, liberty, and property subject to the law of the land. William Blackstone interpreted Coke's "law of the land" to require a two-tier process before a person could be deprived of life or liberty. The vote by the grand jury to determine whether there was probable cause to believe that the accused was guilty of the crime charged; and, the vote by the petit jury to establish if there was enough evidence to convict.

The English law establishing common law grand juries ceased to function in 1933 and was entirely abolished in 1948. Its function was gradually made redundant by the development of a preliminary-type proceedings in magistrates' courts from 1848. Today the British use a committal procedure.

During the early history of the United States, grand juries were used relating to matters involving the public at large. Citizens could bring before a grand jury matters such as a public work needing repair, misconduct by a public official, or a complaint of a crime by a citizen. Grand juries were able to conduct their own investigations. During this period in history, most criminal prosecutions were conducted by private parties. The general public could bring a bill of indictment to the grand jury, and if the grand jury found probable cause, proper jurisdiction, and that the conduct was a crime, it would return an indictment. The grand jury would then appoint the complaining party to prosecute the case, but would screen out incompetent or malicious prosecutions. Later, the addition of public prosecutors did away with these private prosecutions.

The first use of the grand jury in the American colonies started back in 1635. During the American Revolution, grand juries became common since they stood between American patriots and the government prosecutors. In 1791, when the grand jury was incorporated into our constitutional structure, its primary role was to protect individuals from unfounded accusations made by the government.

Why the System Is Outdated

Federal grand juries were intended to be used to sort through weak cases and to protect the accused from overzealous prosecutors. However, things have changed dramatically. Today, federal prosecutors manipulate these grand jury proceedings to present misleading and inadmissible evidence and withhold evidence that favors defendants in order to get their indictments. In fact, federal prosecutors get their indictments in almost all cases. According to the National Association of Criminal Defense Lawyers, "From fiscal years 1994 through 1998, federal prosecutors secured 122,879 indictments" but "failed to get indictments in only 83 cases."[133]

Today, the federal grand jury has become a secret ex parte proceeding behind closed doors where the prosecutor presents evidence of his or her choosing and makes arguments to convince the grand jury to indict the individual who is the target of the prosecutor. Prosecutors get to pick which witnesses will testify and what evidence will be presented to the grand jury. They frame their presentation and argue to grand jurors to charge an individual even without rebuttal from the targeted individual's attorney.

It seems the theory in keeping the grand jury proceedings secret is to protect witnesses from possible intimidation or tampering and to make it more difficult for witnesses to avoid a subpoena requiring them to appear to testify or hide or destroy evidence, or for a defendant to evade arrest. On the other hand, this secret proceeding results in grand jurors seeing only what the prosecutor presents to them. Because there is no one from the defense to contest the prosecutor's argument and evidence, grand juries almost always return an indictment.

Although prosecutors are required to present grand jurors with exculpatory evidence, very few do. Unscrupulous federal prosecutors can easily use this one-sided legal proceeding to their advantage in securing charges against the innocent person.

Consequently, today's federal grand jury is just a rubber stamp for the federal prosecutor, leading many observers to feel that a "good prosecutor could get a grand jury to indict a ham sandwich."[134]

Calls for Reform

There are many who have long been calling for reform of our federal grand jury system, among them many judges, politicians, prosecutors, defense lawyers, professors, and other distinguished U.S. citizens. In response, in May 2000 the National Association of Criminal Defense Lawyers (NACDL) arranged a bipartisan blue-ribbon panel that included defense attorneys, academics, and even current and former prosecutors. The conclusion and proposal for grand jury reform from this diverse group of criminal justice system professionals is contained in the publication "Federal Grand Jury Reform Report & Bill of Rights."[135] This document is summarized as follows:

1. A witness before the grand jury who has not received immunity shall have the right to be accompanied by counsel in his or her appearance before the grand jury.

2. No prosecutor shall knowingly fail to disclose to the federal grand jury evidence in the prosecutor's possession which exonerates the target or subject of the offense.

3. The prosecutor shall not present to the federal grand jury evidence which he or she knows to be constitutionally inadmissible at trial because of a court ruling on the matter.

4. A target or subject of a grand jury investigation shall have the right to testify before the grand jury.

5. Witnesses should have the right to receive a transcript of their federal grand jury testimony.

6. The federal grand jury shall not name a person in an indictment as an unindicted co-conspirator to a criminal conspiracy.

7. All non-immunized subjects or targets called before a federal grand jury shall be given a Miranda warning by the prosecutor before being questioned.

8. All subpoenas for witnesses called before a federal grand jury shall be issued at least seventy-two hours before the date of appearance, not to include weekends and holidays, unless good cause is shown for an exemption.

9. The federal grand jurors shall be given meaningful jury instructions, on the record, regarding their duties and powers as grand jurors, and the charges they are to consider.

10. No prosecutor shall call before the federal grand jury any subject or target who has stated personally or through his attorney that he intends to invoke the constitutional privilege against self-incrimination.[136]

Although to date, there has not been a grand jury reform bill passed and enacted into law, the need for reform has never been greater. It is essential to curtail the continued abuse of our grand jury system that happens throughout the United States every day.

Grand Jury Abuses

The following are some real-life examples of how federal prosecutors abuse the grand jury process to win indictments.

In January 1996, U.S. District Judge Norma L. Shapiro, senior district court judge for the Eastern District of Pennsylvania, scolded prosecutors for engaging in misconduct before a grand jury that included the following: prosecutors told jurors that they did not need to agree with everything stated in the indictment; they brought doughnuts for the grand jurors; and they told the grand jury that they need not be concerned if there was no evidence to support unimportant points. The indictment was dismissed.[137]

In May 1988, John Williams, Jr., a Tulsa, Oklahoma investor, was indicted by a federal grand jury for allegedly making false statements with the intent to influence the actions of a financial institution. The indictment was based on the claim that he overstated his assets and interest income to influence the bank's decision on a loan application. However, according to the district court, the prosecutor failed to present substantial exculpatory evidence to the grand jury that undermined the contention that Williams had taken action with criminal intent—i.e., that he intentionally misled the bank. The exculpatory evidence was his ledger, tax returns, and testimony during his bankruptcy, all entirely consistent with the documents submitted to the bank.[138]

Record-promoter and label-owner Joseph Isgro was arrested in March 2000 for his alleged involvement in a scheme to pay off officials at local radio stations to promote certain musicians. The government's main witness before the grand jury was Dennis DiRicco, an attorney and accountant who had allegedly conspired with Isgro. DiRicco had himself been previously convicted on money laundering and narcotics charges and had testified at his own trial. When DiRicco testified before the grand jury investigating Isgro, his testimony was diametrically opposed to that of his prior trial testimony. The government had a copy of DiRicco's previous trial testimony but never told the grand jury that his testimony was now different or even that the previous transcript existed. The district court dismissed the indictment, but the Ninth Circuit "reluctantly" reversed it, finding that "dismissal of an indictment, particularly with prejudice, is a drastic measure" and that "dismissing the indictment is simply an unwarranted 'windfall' to the defendants."[139]

Robert DiBernardo was indicted for conspiracy to commit interstate transportation of obscene material. The defendants were tried in groups. When over half of the cases had been tried, the government disclosed that one of the FBI agents who had worked undercover posing as a pornographer was arrested for shoplifting and had given his undercover name to the arresting officers. Doctors testified that the agent had difficulty differentiating his real identity from his undercover identity. Moreover, the prosecutor knew of the agent's psychological problems before he testified in the grand jury. The court dismissed the indictments against all remaining defendants.[140]

These are just a few examples of the kind of prosecutorial misconduct that goes on behind the closed doors of a grand jury room. Unfortunately, there are hundreds of cases just like these.

According to the American Bar Association, "No prosecutor should knowingly fail to disclose to the grand jury evidence which tends to negate guilt or mitigate the offence."[141] In my case, my attorney never did look into my grand jury proceedings to determine if there had been any misconduct in this regard. All the evidence presented in Chapter 16 of this book was undoubtedly in the possession of federal prosecutors, but I bet it was not presented to the grand jury.

Chapter 19

Prosecutorial Abuse

I N 1999, THE *Pittsburg Post-Gazette* published a ten-part investigative series about the misconduct of federal prosecutors titled "Win at All Costs" that was published in January 1999. Reporter Bill Moushey stated the following:

> Hundreds of times during the past ten years, federal agents and prosecutors have pursued justice by breaking the law. They lied, hid evidence, distorted facts, engaged in cover-ups, paid for perjury and set up innocent people in a relentless effort to win indictments, guilty pleas and convictions . . .
>
> Rarely were these federal officials punished for their misconduct. Rarely did they admit their conduct was wrong.
>
> New laws and court rulings that encourage federal law enforcement officers to press the boundaries of their power while providing few safeguards against abuse fueled their actions.

Victims of this misconduct sometimes lost their jobs, assets and even families. Some remain in prison because prosecutors withheld favorable evidence or allowed fabricated testimony. Some criminals walk free as a reward for conspiring with the government in its effort to deny others their rights.[142]

A decade later, in 2010, *USA Today* investigated and documented 201 criminal cases throughout our nation in which federal judges found that federal prosecutors broke the rules. In an article titled "Prosecutors' Conduct Can Tip Justice Scales," reporters Brad Heath and Kevin McCoy found that prosecutors repeatedly violated their duty to seek justice and instead put innocent people in prison and let guilty people free, costing taxpayers millions of dollars in legal fees and sanctions. According to this article, in case after case, many different judges blasted prosecutors for flagrant and outrageous misconduct, such as hiding evidence and lying to judges and juries.[143]

The article further states the following:

USA Today found a pattern of "serious, glaring misconduct," said Pace University law professor Bennett Gershman, an expert on misconduct by prosecutors. "It's systemic now, and . . . the system is not able to control this type of behavior. There is no accountability."

He and Alexander Bunin, the chief federal public defender in Albany, NY, called the newspaper's findings "the tip of the iceberg" because many more cases are tainted by misconduct than are found. In many cases, misconduct is exposed only because of vigilant scrutiny by defense attorneys and judges.

In a justice system that prosecutes more than 60,000 people a year, mistakes are inevitable. But the violations *USA Today* documented go beyond everyday missteps. In the worst cases, say judges, former prosecutors and others, they happen because prosecutors deliberately cut corners to win.

"There are rogue prosecutors, often motivated by personal ambition or partisan reasons," said Thornburgh, who was attorney general under Presidents Reagan and George H.W. Bush. Such people are uncommon, though, he added: "Most former federal prosecutors, like myself, are resentful of actions that bring discredit on the office."

Judges have seen those abuses, too. "Sometimes, you get inexperienced and unscrupulous assistant U.S. attorneys who don't care about the rules," said U.W. Clemon, the former chief judge in northern Alabama's federal courts.

How often prosecutors deliberately violate the rules is impossible to know. The Justice Department's internal ethics watchdog, the Office of Professional Responsibility, insists it happens rarely. It reported that it completed more than 750 investigations over the past decade and found intentional violations in just sixty-eight. The department would not identify the cases it concluded were marred by intentional violations, and removes from its public reports any details that could be used to identify the prosecutors involved.

USA Today went on to publish a series of articles addressing prosecutorial misconduct that was recognized by the Sidney Hillman Foundation for "Exemplary Reporting that Fosters Social and Economic Justice."[144] Perhaps due to the publicity of these articles, in January 2011, the DOJ announced the creation of a new unit whose sole mission would be to discipline federal prosecutors who have broken ethics rules. According to a memorandum from Attorney General Eric Holder dated January 14, 2011, the Professional Misconduct Review Unit (PMRU) was established to "facilitate timely, fair, and consistent resolution of disciplinary matters arising out of findings of professional misconduct by the Office of Professional Responsibility (OPR) . . ."[145]

It's obvious that the press is becoming more and more aware of this misconduct that takes place in our federal system and in turn is informing the general public about these abuses. But still, more journalists need to expose this misconduct which I fear continues on.

Absolute Immunity

While I believe the majority of federal prosecutors are ethical lawyers who engage in a vital public service, the irrefutable fact is that many innocent people have been wrongly convicted of federal crimes as a result of prosecutorial misconduct. As it turns out, these federal prosecutors who commit such transgressions are seldom disciplined or criminally prosecuted for their misdeeds.

Federal prosecutors are protected from civil lawsuits even though they engage in such conduct as hiding exculpatory evidence, fabricating evidence, coercing witnesses to testify falsely, and knowingly using false or misleading testimony during trial. Not even when their conduct results in the conviction and incarceration of an innocent person can they be sued. Back in the 1970s, in *Imbler v. Pachtman*, the Supreme Court held that prosecutors cannot face civil lawsuits over how they handled a case no matter how serious the abuse.[146] Since that time, courts have further limited the circumstances under which a prosecutor can be sued for civil rights violations.

The rationale for this prosecutorial protection, as expressed by the Supreme Court in the *Imbler* decision, is that because a prosecutor's workload requires numerous decisions that may give rise to legitimate constitutional claims, not only would an accused prosecutor be distracted from his principal duty of law enforcement, but defending such claims, perhaps years after alleged conduct took place, would also impose "intolerable burdens" upon both the prosecutor and the criminal justice system.[147] As noted by the Supreme Court, the proper functioning of the criminal justice system requires that a prosecutor have wide-ranging discretion in presenting the government's case. The likelihood of possible personal liability from a post-trial lawsuit might persuade the prosecutor to manage witnesses or evidence in such a way that would deny the jury potential relevant evidence or avoid a trial all together.[148]

Nevertheless, protecting the dishonest federal prosecutor at the expense of the innocent victim takes away the purpose of the civil rights legislation in the first place by failing to deter prosecutorial misconduct. In other words, if a federal prosecutor knows that his conduct, no matter how dishonest and corrupt, protects him or her from the consequences of personal liability or even criminal prosecution, then the unscrupulous federal prosecutor will do whatever is necessary to win his or her case.

Unfortunately, reforming the criminal justice system is difficult to accomplish. Politicians continue to pass more and more laws with stiffer sentences to support their tough-on-crime rhetoric. In turn, prosecutors use these new laws to leverage plea bargains. For these bureaucrats, this is a win–win proposition but a tragedy for the innocent who find themselves caught up in a unfair and self-serving system.

Chapter 20

Prosecutorial Advantage

F OR MANY REASONS, federal prosecutors have a tremendous advantage against innocent individuals falsely accused of crimes. These advantages include their tactic of overcharging (piling on "counts" that all relate to the same conduct); their ability to use the media to create public bias against defendants; the fact that jurors are already biased in favor of the prosecution and don't understand the concept of "presumed innocence"; and, finally, the fact that it is in the interest of defense attorneys to get their clients to plead out rather than fight at trial.

Although our Constitution clearly spells out that once you are accused of a crime you are innocent until proven guilty, that is just not the mindset that operates in the real world. Due to the prejudice inherent in our criminal justice system, once you are accused, in the eyes of criminal administrators and even jurors you are labled guilty until you prove your innocence. I believed that, as a defense strategy, it is more effective to operate based on the idea that you will be viewed as guilty until proven innocent. That way, the innocent criminal defendant will not be lulled into thinking that a simple showing of reasonable doubt will save him rather than having to prove that he did not commit the crime for which he is accused.

Overcharging

One tactic used by federal prosecutors to create prejudice against the target of a prosecution, whether guilty or innocent, is to pile on as many criminal counts as possible for fundamentally the same alleged criminal conduct. This works to a prosecutor's advantage since the more counts added to an indictment the more the perception of jurors is swayed against the defendant.

As an example, I am aware of an individual who was convicted on all counts in a 150-count indictment. All of these counts were essentially related to the same alleged crime. When you added up his sentence according to the federal statutes—five years for each count—his statutory sentence, if consecutive, would have been 750 years. However, according to the Federal Sentencing Guidelines, his sentence was calculated at only six years, which was the sentence he received. This was due to the fact that the Sentencing Guidelines are used by federal judges to determine a convicted individual's ultimate sentence. The total of the sentence (in this case 750 years) only acts as a statutory sentencing maximum in the event that the guidelines or the courts' reasonable discretion reaches that high. Prosecutors could have theoretically sought an indictment for just five counts, and this defendant most likely would have received the same sentence (six years) since all of the alleged conduct for the remaining 145 counts would have been admitted by prosecutors during his sentencing. But of course federal prosecutors know that when jurors are presented with a 150-count indictment they are thinking that with all these counts, this guy must have done what the government claims. This overcharging tactic used by federal prosecutors can undoubtedly influence the perception of both the grand jury and the jurors at trial toward an innocent individual.

In my case, the government took the $20,752 in 401(k) funds allegedly converted and divided them up over five counts. Count 5 was $7,163; count 6 was $7,379; count 7 was $2,460; count 8 was $3,011, and count 9 was $739. Obviously, these five counts could have easily been rolled into one, but then the prosecutor would not have gotten the shock value it needed to help win its case.

The Public Relations Machine

Almost immediately after an individual or company is indicted, a public relations person in the Department of Justice, and perhaps in whatever other federal agency was involved, issues a press release regarding the allegations specific to the indictment. These press releases are sent to all local media in that district in addition to being published on the agency's Website.

Although the government would argue that the intent of these press releases is to inform the public about the work they are doing at their behest, I believe that there is a much more sinister motive at play here. I believe prosecutors are attempting to affect public perception of the innocent defendant and perhaps negatively influence the jury pool.

In my case, a Department of Labor press release was sent out to all local newspapers, in turn each ran lengthy stories based on the government's propaganda. In fact, many of these stories ended up on the front page of the business section. In addition, one of the three major TV stations in Milwaukee showed up at my front door one evening with lights blazing and cameras rolling in an attempt to get their story. I was in my car when I received a frantic call from my wife. "There are cameras and lights from

Channel 6 at our front door. What should I do?" I told her not to answer the door since I was sure the reporter would ambush her with questions she was unable to answer. They soon went away. That evening, sure enough my indictment was the top story on the local newscast.

Obviously, I was told by my attorney not to say anything or conduct any interviews. Nevertheless, the government was able to get its version of events out to the public, which unquestionably affected the attitudes of local citizens exposed to these news stories.

Jurors Are Naturally Biased Against Defendants

Today, the law requires that jurors swear under oath that they can put aside what they personally believe and have read or heard about a case and presume that the individual on trial is innocent unless or until the government can prove the person is guilty. But, as a practical matter, I believe that jurors have a tendency toward assuming guilt even before they hear the first piece of evidence on the first day of trial.

According to a January 2006 *Houston Chronicle* article titled "The Fall of Enron: Swearing the Oath to Presumed Innocence," Houston defense attorney Joel Androphy said he thinks the words "presumption of innocence" has "zero value" these days. "People hear the term, but when they come into the courtroom, they think the government would not go through this if there weren't something there," he said. "They think the grand jury and an indictment mean guilt. The average person doesn't know and understand the system, and people draw conclusions very quickly."[149]

Defendants who have been the subject of local and/or national publicity are especially disadvantaged. Steve Sheppard, a University of Arkansas School of Law professor who has written on the presumption of innocence, believes pre-trial media coverage makes it increasingly difficult to find open-minded jurors.[150]

Adding further to jurors' perhaps unintended prejudice toward the defendant is their belief in the prestige of the U.S. Attorney's Office and the common knowledge of the extent of the government's investigatory resources. This notion helps support the view that federal prosecutors would not proceed criminally against an individual unless they were certain of the commission of a crime.

In my case, the selected jurors swore under oath that they would maintain a "presumption of innocence" throughout my trial, which included the court's instructions that "[a] defendant is presumed to be innocent of each of these charges" and that "[t]his presumption continues during every stage of the trial, and in your deliberations on the verdict."[151] However, according to Edward J. Bronson, a leading expert on jury behavior and professor emeritus of political science at California State University, "[d]ecades of social science teach that most people have great difficulty identifying their own prejudices, and even among those who do, all but a few underreport their existence and overestimate their ability to control them."[152]

Also in my case, jurors were questioned as an entire group about their ability to be fair and impartial during my trial. However, this group's questioning by the court really does nothing to weed out potential jurors who think otherwise. According to Bronson, "social science research . . . teaches us that direct questions to the whole panel on fairness issues are not likely to be productive. Greater insight can be gained by questioning jurors individually, or at least in small panels. For many panel members, especially those whose questionnaire responses are problematic, sequestered *voir dire* is a much better approach to identify bias.

Not only does social science research support individualized, isolated *voir dire* to encourage forthcoming answers and prevent other jurors from learning what the "correct" responses are, but it avoids contaminating the entire panel.[153]

Clearly, federal prosecutors are fully aware of the extent to which jurors are biased against defendants.

Jurors Don't Understand Reasonable Doubt

The reasonable doubt standard is the central feature of our criminal justice system. This standard represents society's belief that no person should be convicted of a crime unless the fact-finder is nearly certain of that person's guilt.[154] In criminal prosecutions, the jurors must use the reasonable doubt standard as a filter through which to sift the evidence and determine whether to acquit or convict.

In some federal districts in this country, the judge will give the jury a definition of "reasonable doubt." However, studies have shown that juries fail to comprehend key instructions.[155] This failure to comprehend can prevent a jury from correctly applying jury instructions and can deny a defendant the constitutionally guaranteed protection of the reasonable doubt standard.

Making things worse, some jurisdictions don't even attempt to explain the concept to jurors. For example, the Seventh Circuit Court Committee that governs the Southeastern District Court of Wisconsin, where my case was tried, *recommends that no instructions be given defining "reasonable doubt."* According to the court, "the phrase reasonable doubt is self-explanatory and is its own best definition. Further elaboration tends to misleading refinements that weaken and make imprecise the existing phase. A judge should not define the term for the jury even if asked to do so during deliberations" (internal quotes omitted).[156]

This omission leaves jurors without any understanding of "reasonable doubt," which can be problematic for the defendant. Moreover, this so-called "higher standard of proof," a standard of proof supposedly much higher than other legal standands— such as the "preponderance of evidence" standard used in civil cases—is in reality not a higher standard in terms of protecting the innocent if jurors don't understand its meaning or even how it should be measured against the admitted evidence. Federal prosecutors understand that jurors are confused by the term "reasonable doubt" and that most jury deliberations never put the government's case to this higher standard which in turn allows for the conviction of an innocent individual.

Ineffective Defense Counsel

Where most federal criminal defendants make their first fatal mistake is in selecting the wrong attorney to represent them. I can't emphasize this enough. Indeed, in any given area there are only a few lawyers whom you'd want to hire if you were going to fight rather than plead.

Many criminal defense attorneys are what are known in the legal profession as "dump truck lawyers": they promise a strong defense but do very little investigative work and encourage clients to plead out to save themselves the trouble of preparing for trial. In fact, once they get your retainer, they file a few boilerplate pretrial motions and then work on convincing you to plead out even before they have thoroughly investigated your case.

Why would your attorney do this to you? For a few reasons. Such lawyers generally charge a flat fee and sell you on the idea that this is all you will have to pay for your pre-trial investigation even if they spend much more time on your case than anticipated. Then they will do very little, if any, investigating, let you cool off, and tactfully persuade you to plead out, thereby keeping the flat fee for very little work.

According to the U.S. Sentencing Commission's 2010 data, 96.8% of all individuals indicted by the federal government plead out instead of going to trial.[157] This process of pleading out saves the U.S. Attorney's Office and the federal court's resources, since trial preparation by the government and federal court time can take weeks or even months. If defense attorneys throughout our country collectively brought more of their clients' cases to trial, forcing the government to prove their cases, the U.S. Attorney's criminal division and the federal court system would come to a screeching halt and so would the dump truck lawyers' income. In other words, no one wants to mess with the hen that lays the golden eggs.

This practice of dump truck lawyering provides federal prosecutors with many more convictions of innocent people than would otherwise occur, since a plea bargain is a conviction with only about a day in court for the defendant.

In my case, at my very first meeting with my defense attorney, right after my indictment, he recited from the Federal Sentencing Guidelines the extent of my prison term in the event I were to be convicted at trial even before we discussed the details of my case. I felt his approach was to scare me so that I would just tell him to go to the prosecutor and get me a better deal, which is standard procedure.

If you do end up, like me, among the 3.2% of indicted individuals who go to trial, you are much more likely to be among the approximately eighty-five percent who are convicted rather than the fifteen percent that go free. If you are convicted before a judge or jury, be prepared to be severely punished with long-term incarceration at your sentencing for exercising your constitutional right by putting the government through a trial. In fact in 2010, the U.S. Sentencing Commission Data shows that approximately ninety-five percent of all defendants who were convicted in federal court went to prison.[158]

As you can see, the innocent defendant really face a substantial uphill battle just to even the playing field with the federal prosecutor. But once you understand the substantial advantages the prosecutor maintains, you will be able to take the appropriate action to, with any luck, negate some of the government's benefits. Know thine enemy—that's the best advice I can give. Once you understand what is really going on around you and you find an attorney who is *truly* on your side, only then can you work with your lawyer to give you, the innocent defendant, the best odds of winning the freedom you will undoubtedly soon be losing.

Chapter 21

Overcriminalization

B OBBY UNSER, the three-time Indy 500 winner, was convicted of a federal crime for getting lost in a blizzard and inadvertently entering a U.S. wilderness area.

Abner Schoenwetter, a successful seafood importer, was sentenced to eight years in a federal prison for importing lobsters in the U.S. in violation of Honduran Fishing Regulations despite the fact none of these regulations were valid at the time.

Eddie Anderson, a retired logger and former science teacher, is now a federal convict because he loaned his son some tools to dig for arrowheads near their favorite campsite. Unfortunately for him, he was unacquainted with the Archaeological Resource Protections Act of 1976, which does not require a finding of criminal intent to put him in a federal penitentiary.

Federal prosecutors have charged many individuals under the "honest services" fraud statute punishable by up to twenty years in prison. In one example, Kevin Geddings, a well-known

Democratic political consultant and former chief of staff to Governor Jim Hodges of South Carolina, was tried and convicted of honest service fraud. The law prohibits politicians from secretly enriching themselves from official actions. In this case, the charges against Geddings state that he did not disclose that he had received $250,000 from a lottery vendor at the time he accepted an appointment to the new state lottery commission in 2005. At trial, state ethics officials testified that Geddings should have disclosed his financial ties before he joined the commission. The jury convicted him on five counts of honest service mail fraud and the court sentenced him to forty-eight months in federal prison. Geddings continued to maintain his innocence and fought his conviction all the way to the Supreme Court, which declined to hear his case.

Then, finally, during its 2009-10 term, there were three appeals against the honest services fraud statute all challenging its constitutionality. In June 2010, the Supreme Court stepped in to put a stop to this insanity by ruling that this criminal law was unconstitutionally vague. On June 29, 2010, after Geddings had been in federal prison for nearly three years, Judge James Dever III ordered him to be immediately released.

These real-life horror stories are the result of overzealous prosecutors using our nation's vague and ambiguous non-violent criminal laws to convict individuals for largely benign conduct that lacks true criminal intent and that, at most, warrants a civil action by a federal regulatory agency.

The core standard of our American justice system is that citizens should not be subjected to criminal prosecution and conviction unless they deliberately engage in illegal conduct they *know* to be unlawful. Absent an obvious connection between an individual's conduct and his mental culpability, criminal laws nevertheless subject the innocent to unfair prosecution and punishment for honest mistakes or actions that they had no reason to believe were against the law.

Over the past several years, the federal government has increasingly employed criminal statutes in its attempt to control behavior. Congress has invoked this tremendous power of government—the power to prosecute and imprison—as a regulatory device, something never contemplated by our nation's founders. By the end of 2007, the U.S. Code—the official compilation of the federal laws currently in force—included over 4,000 federal crimes; an estimated tens of thousands more are located in the federal regulatory code.

Nevertheless, something essential is often lacking from this surge of punitive laws: meaningful *mens rea* requirements. *Mens rea* is a Latin term referring to a culpable mental state. Absent this mental state, there is no crime.

Unfortunately, Congress has enacted scores of laws with weak, confusing, or even no *mens rea* requirements, the result of a legislative process that is disorganized and unpredictable. In doing so, it has eroded the principle of fair notice and dangerously impaired the justification for criminal punishment that has for centuries been based on a person's intent to commit an illegal act. This trend undermines confidence in our federal government and risks persistent injustice.

In an April 2010 report titled, "Without Intent: How Congress Is Eroding the Criminal Intent Requirement in Federal Law," the Heritage Foundation provides five specific recommendations to begin to solve the problem of overcriminalization of our country's laws. Congress should:

1. Enact default rules of interpretation to ensure that *mens rea* requirements are adequate to protect against unjust conviction.

2. Codify the common-law rule of lenity, which grants defendants the benefit of doubt when Congress fails to legislate clearly.

3. Require judiciary committee oversight of every bill that includes criminal offenses or penalties.

4. Require detailed written justification for and analysis of all new federal criminalization.

5. Draft every criminal offense with clarity and precision.

According to the report, out of 446 studied criminal offenses, 255, or fifty-seven percent, had either very weak or no *mens rea* requirements.

Three Felonies a Day: How the Feds Target the Innocent by Harvey A. Silvergate (Encounter, 2009) covers the topic of overcriminalization in depth. Silvergate says the following:

> The average professional in this country wakes up in the morning, goes to work, comes home, eats dinner, and then goes to sleep, unaware that he or she has likely committed several federal criminal laws that day. Why? The answer lies in the very nature of modern federal criminal laws, which have exploded in numbers but also become impossibly broad and vague . . . The volume of federal crimes in recent decades has increased well beyond the statute books and into the morass of the Code of Federal

Regulations, handing federal prosecutors an additional trove of vague and exceedingly complex and technical prohibitions to stick on their hapless targets . . .

No social class or profession is safe from this troubling form of social control by the executive branch, and nothing less than the integrity of our constitutional democracy hangs in the balance.[159]

So how is it possible to unknowingly have committed a federal crime? First, the criminal laws enacted by Congress start off generalized and vague. This allows the enforcers of our federal criminal laws—federal prosecutors—to link them to individual conduct, at their discretion, that Congress never intended to make criminal. Here are a few examples:

The Stolen Valor Act of 2005, which was enacted into law in December 2006, is an example of a typical weak *mens rea* criminal law. Under this act, it is a federal crime to "knowingly" buy, sell, mail, ship, barter a wide variety of military decorations, badges, and medals. The purpose of this law was to prevent fraudulent use of or claims about U.S. military decorations such as falsely claiming to be the recipient of the Congressional Medal of Honor or Purple Heart. But this law was written so broadly by Congress, and with a very weak *mens rea* requirement, that it could risk imprisonment for legitimate historians and collectors of these military decorations and even the heirs of soldiers who choose to transfer these medals between themselves. The Stolen Valor Act's only *mens rea* requirement is that a person charged must have "knowingly" engaged in the prohibited act. As the Supreme Court has held, unless the text of the statute states a different result, the term "knowingly" simply requires proof of knowledge of the facts that constitute the offense.[160] In addition, the term "knowingly" does not necessarily have any reference to a "culpable state of mind or to knowledge of the law."[161] Therefore, this offense created by the Stolen Valor Act does not provide sufficient protection against a criminal prosecution and punishment for individuals who buy, sell, exchange, or ship military decoration, badges, or medals without any intention of committing a crime.

The Federal Mineral Development and Land Protection Equity Act of 2005 also contains a weak criminal intent requirement. Under this act, it is a federal crime to "knowingly" violate any other environmental protection requirement set forth in this act, any regulation issued pursuant to this act, or any permit published under this act. Clearly, this law's criminal intent (*mens rea*) prerequisite "knowingly" requires the government to prove the conduct was not an accident or inadvertent, but the definition of "knowingly" again does not require "a culpable state of mind or knowledge of the law."[162]

This again provides very little protection to those who are unaware of the law or those individuals who, in good faith, try to comply with this law but are unable to do so.

As you can see, overciminalization is a real problem in this country. While many violent crimes go unpunished, Congress continues to concoct new criminal offenses out of more or less ordinary conduct. Today, there are thousands of federal criminal laws and even more that are contained in federal regulations. In this day and age, it is very easy for any business person to be hauled off to a federal prison for conduct that no reasonable person would consider a crime.

Chapter 22

How Prosecutors Win Against the Innocent

A FEW FEDERAL PROSECUTORS who choose to use their position with the Department of Justice to convict individuals, by way of misconduct and other illegal means, know just how to win their cases no matter if a person they targeted is guilty or innocent.

Many times these prosecutors are motivated by a desire for career advancement since every conviction, length of sentence, and total dollars involved are points in the prosecutor's favor. Perhaps a belief that they are doing "God's work" allows them to sleep at night when they knowingly have engaged in reprehensible misconduct to secure a conviction.

These federal prosecutors know their advantages and exploit the federal criminal justice system and all its elements to win their cases regardless if the person who has unfortunately ended up in their crosshairs is innocent. Over the next several chapters, I will present what I believe to be clear and persuasive evidence to convince you that an innocent person really does not stand a chance once he or she enters our federal criminal justice system.

Manipulating Access to Evidence

One of the most effective ways by which unscrupulous prosecutors can actually frame innocent people and win convictions is by restricting the defendant's access to evidence in the government's possession that demonstrates doubt as to guilt. As a guard against false convictions, the U.S. Supreme Court recognized a defendant's right to this "discovery evidence" information in its 1963 ruling in *Brady v. Maryland*.[163]

The investigative resources of the government are greater than those available to most private citizens, which often enables the government to unearth exculpatory evidence—undiscovered by the defense—that can undermine the government's case. The government might, for example, unearth a document implicating someone other than its target.

This situation creates an irresistible temptation for prosecutors across this nation to thumb their noses at the Supreme Court and at the rights of all Americans by hiding the existence of evidence that would interfere with their convicting an accused person. These prosecutors know full well that they are immune from lawsuits and that their employer, the Department of Justice, rarely if ever severely reprimands prosecutors. Ironically, this means that innocent people are rarely helped by the pre-trial discovery process because it is in the personal and professional interest of prosecutors to conceal potentially exonerating information from them.

There are numerous cases of wrongful convictions known to have been orchestrated by the concealment of evidence by prosecutors. These cases span the length and breadth of the country and include state and federal courts.

One of the more famous examples was what happened during the prosecution of Alaska Senator Ted Stevens, which I will discuss in greater detail in the next chapter. An independent investigation found that the prosecution concealed evidence that would have helped Stevens defend himself at this 2008 trial. In another case, U.S. District Court Judge A. Howard Matz overturned a bribery conviction against two executives from the Lindsey Manufacturing Company because the government had failed to hand over grand jury testimony.[164]

In addition to withholding evidence, some of the more popular and effective techniques prosecutors use to frame defendants are:

- They permit, encourage, compel, or purchase perjurious testimony in court by prosecution witnesses. In Ellen Reasonover's case, for example, the prosecution paid cash for the testimony of one witness and rewarded another witness by dropping felony charges against her. In 1993, Ms. Reasonover called police to report information she thought might help regarding a murder near St. Louis. However, she soon found herself charged, tried and convicted of that murder.

- They permit or encourage the introduction of tainted or phony evidence in court. This can be done by introducing tests conducted on contaminated physical evidence, introducing fake evidence, or introducing planted objects as authentic.

- They make unsupported, disparaging, and inflammatory remarks about a defendant and the motives of the defense lawyer so that jurors will have an emotional, rather than rational response, and want to convict a defendant the prosecution hasn't proved to be guilty beyond a reasonable doubt.

Although such prosecutorial tactics are regularly recognized by courts as deplorable, that doesn't stop defendants from being framed by prosecutors. This is due in large part to the narrow interpretation by courts of what is known as the "harmless error" rule. If a prosecutorial tactic isn't considered sufficient in and of itself to have altered the outcome of a trial, it is dismissed by courts as a "harmless error." Therefore, prosecutors know that as long as they use tactics to frame a defendant that aren't excessively obvious or prejudicial of their rights, these won't be deemed a sufficient reason to reverse a conviction or even prompt a judicial reprimand.[165]

By Misusing Evidence

Unethical federal prosecutors will do pretty much anything to win their case, legal or otherwise. This includes attempting to get admitted at trial a defendant's personal assets and income information in hopes of using such evidence in a prejudicial way to create a class bias with jurors. Many times, perhaps when prosecutors know defense counsel is not that sharp, they will argue to the court that a certain piece of evidence should be admitted making representations that this evidence is necessary in proving their case. Once this evidence is admitted, they use it in such a way to create only prejudice against the defendant.

As I described in earlier chapters, in my case, my attorney filed a pre-trial motion asking the court not to allow the government to admit my personal income and asset information since it could be used against me in a prejudicial way by government. During the court hearing regarding this motion, the government argued that it needed this evidence to demonstrate that I had looted my companies through payments to myself of significant compensation, which I then used to purchase personal assets.

Therefore, this would show, according to the government, my motive and intent in deliberately stealing employee ERISA funds.

After the court allowed this evidence to be presented to the jury, the government did admit evidence that I received compensation (although they never established it was excessive) and that I owned some personal assets. However, they never provided any proof that any of my income was used to purchase any of my personal assets. In fact, all my personal assets were purchased well before the relevant time that the government claimed I had committed the alleged crimes.

Instead of using this evidence for the purpose they claimed they would use it for, they used it to successfully argue that I should have used my personal assets to pay employees' unpaid health claims—yet I was not even charged with failure to pay the health claims. This was clearly an example of lying to the court with complete disregard for the court's evidentiary ruling, and the deliberate misuse of this evidence in front of jurors demonstrating just how far federal prosecutors are willing to go in their efforts to win a case.

Getting Witnesses to Lie

It's one thing to get caught lying to your wife about what you think about her new dress, it's quite another thing to lie in federal court. If you get caught, the consequences are much steeper. Lying in federal court can cost you five years in prison plus fines. It's called perjury. However, this potential penalty does not seem to deter many witnesses from lying in federal court. Telling one lie usually means that you have to tell a bunch of other lies in order for your story to be consistent.

Monroe H. Freedman, a law professor at Hofstra University and former dean of Hofstra LawSchool, covered the topic of lying witnesses in his 2010 article titled "The Cooperating Witness Who Lies—A Challenge to Defense Lawyers, Prosecutors, and Judges," published in *Ohio State Journal of Criminal Law*. Freedman states the following:

> According to the United States Department of Justice, many cooperating witnesses are "outright conscience-less sociopaths" who will do anything to benefit themselves, including "lying, committing perjury, manufacturing evidence, soliciting others to corroborate their lies with more lies, and double-crossing anyone with whom they come into contact."

> Nevertheless, prosecutors commonly encourage and use cooperating witnesses, and not surprisingly, this practice has resulted in a significant number of wrongful convictions.[166]

Moreover, it seems that government witnesses are willing to lie while testifying for the government for many reasons such as having been promised a reduced sentence from the prosecutor for their own criminal conduct; having been personally threatened with prosecution; having had a family member threatened with prosecution; and having been told they will be harassed by other investigations and/or IRS tax audits.

It is well understood in certain legal communities that the government creates the facts and the only way an innocent person can receive justice is to beat them using the law. This notion never made sense to me until I learned just how federal prosecutors essentially create the facts through witnesses and the evidence they selectively provide and manipulate. Federal prosecutors are fully aware of the power they have over witnesses and are often able to either directly or indirectly shape how their witness testifies in court, thus creating facts consistent with their theory of the case. Although federal prosecutors claim that the accuracy of their witness' testimony is challenged by defense counsel's cross-examination, if government witnesses are willing to lie and defense counsel is unable to impeach or rebut these witness' testimony with contrary evidence, the uncorroborated witness' testimony will stand as sufficient direct evidence for the jury to convict.

Delivering Prejudicial Opening and Closing Statements

The opening statement by federal prosecutors, like their counterpart the defense attorneys, are intended to be used to introduce to the jury (or judge in a bench trial), by way of a persuasive and compelling story, the theory of their case and what the evidence will show. Ethics rules governing prosecutors conduct state the following:

> The primary purpose of the opening statement is to give the prosecutor an opportunity to outline the issues and matters he or she believes can and will be supported by competent and admissible evidence introduced during trial. In that statement, the prosecutor should scrupulously avoid any utterance that he or she believes cannot and will not later actually be supported with such evidence.[167]

Nevertheless, certain federal prosecutors are willing to use this opportunity to prejudice the jury against the defendant during their opening statements. In my case, the prosecutor told the jury that "[y]ou will hear testimony from Dale Garber that his medical bills exceed $250,000 and were never paid by Western Rubber at all."[168] As it turned out, Garber never testified and the government never admitted evidence that Western was responsible for any of these medical bills, since Garber was not an employee and had not paid his COBRA premium during the time he incurred these medical bills.[169] A prosecutor is prohibited from referring to evidence unless there is a "good faith and reasonable basis for believing that such evidence will be tendered and admitted in evidence."[170] It is my belief that the prosecutor in my case, Giampietro, mentioned Garber's unpaid healthcare claims and the claim that Western was liable to pay these claims to the jury without any intention of either admitting proof or providing Garber's testimony at trial. This was just another example of how a dishonest prosecutor can prejudice jurors to win his case at all costs.

Closing statements are arguments intended to provide jurors with an overview as to the evidence admitted at trial. Each party can only make arguments related by "reasonable inference" to the evidence in the record. The government goes first, then the defense, and finally, the government makes a final closing argument called the closing rebuttal.

According to ethics rules that govern federal prosecutors' conduct, closing statements are intended to allow the prosecutor to argue to the jury all reasonable inferences from the evidence admitted at trial.[171] Conversely, prosecutors are not allowed to: mis-state the evidence; mislead the jury as to the inferences it may draw; express their personal beliefs as to the truth or falsity of any testimony or evidence or guilt of the defendant; make arguments calculated to appeal to the prejudices of the jury; or make arguments that would divert the jury from its duty to decide the case on the evidence.[172] Nevertheless, this does not stop ruthless and unruly federal prosecutors from violating these rules in an effort to win their case.

In a pivotal case involving, in part, misconduct during closing arguments, the prosecutor, Harry Singer, then chief assistant U.S. attorney in Brooklyn, was found by the Supreme Court to have had "evil influence upon the jury."[173] In 1934, the defendant, Harry Berger, a real estate agent, was indicted with seven others on charges of conspiracy to deal in counterfeit bank notes and for possession of counterfeit bank notes. The charges were based on the testimony of Jack Katz, an accomplice with Berger who had a lengthy criminal record, who testified in exchange for a reduced sentence. The jury acquitted Berger of possessing forged bank notes but convicted him of conspiracy. He was sentenced to a year and a day in federal prison. Berger's attorney appealed the conviction with the Second Circuit Court of Appeals, but it affirmed his conviction.[174] Berger's attorney then filed a petition with the Supreme Court and was granted certiorari.

Although this was a run-of-the-mill federal conspiracy case that raised no constitutional or significant questions of law, this was the first case in which the Supreme Court reviewed a claim whereby a prosecutor had allegedly overstepped the bounds of proper courtroom behavior. The Supreme Court reversed Berger's convictions and found that the prosecutor, Singer, had brutally and relentlessly attacked Berger's character including making a statement to the jury that Berger was a liar, making unjustified insinuations that Berger had engaged in immoral and wrongful behavior, and deliberately making false and inflammatory insinuations about Berger's character that were obviously intended to mislead the jury.

The decision in *Berger* has served as a precedent by which many prosecutorial misconduct cases have been judged.

Actually, there are hundreds of examples of prosecutors using closing arguments to purposely mislead jurors on the evidence. However, rather than recite these numerous cases, I will use my own case to demonstrate what I believe to be clear examples of misconduct. During closing arguments, the federal prosecutors in my case (AUSA Giampietro and AUSA Jacobs) misled jurors several times relating to the evidence admitted at trial. In fact, the government's ability to mislead the jury appeared to be relatively easy since none of the jurors took notes during my week-long trial. I wasn't sure if this was a local court rule or if the jurors were just not very interested in keeping the facts straight. In any event, here are the facts:

During trial, Thresa Palkowsi, Badger's human relations director, testified that she did not intend to mislead employees nor did she believe that I intended to mislead employees by the use of the language "insurance carrier," which the government had alleged in Count 10 was a crime.[175]

However, during closing arguments, AUSA Jacobs put his own "spin" on what he believed Palkowski meant by her testimony when he made the following statement to the jury:

> "[Palkowski] didn't mean to do anything wrong. [Whiting] didn't mean to do anything wrong, because if [Whiting] didn't mean to do anything wrong, then [Palkowski] didn't mean to do anything wrong. To protect myself [Palkowski], I have [to] say [Whiting] didn't mean to do anything wrong."[176]

Just like in the *Berger* case, prosecutors are not supposed to mis-state witness testimony or make statements "containing improper insinuations and assertions calculated to mislead the jury." In fact, prosecutors' own ethics rules prohibit such conduct. According to the ABA, "[e]xpressions of personal opinion by the prosecutor are a form of unsworn, unchecked testimony and tend to exploit the influence of the prosecutor's office and undermine the objective detachment that should separate a lawyer from the cause being argued. Such argument is expressly forbidden by the ABA model ethics codes."[177]

So, when you compare Palkowski's actual testimony to the prosecutor's personal opinion of her testimony, which took place during the final few hours of the trial, you can clearly see what the prosecutor was attempting to accomplish—that is, change jurors' recollection of Palkowski's own testimony (which took place several days earlier). Unfortunately for defendants, this prosecutorial tactic is highly successful but very much illegal and unethical.

Furthermore, during closing arguments, AUSA Jacobs presented evidence that Badger took money from its employees through payroll deductions intended to be used to pay health insurance premiums and argued that "Badger did use it to pay Mr. Whiting."[178] However, there was absolutely no evidence presented at trial that I received any of the employee money. Also, despite the fact that during cross-examination the government's own witness—FBI Agent Sparacino—finally admitted that he could not find even "one dollar" of employee payroll deductions which were paid to Mr. Whiting,[179] Jacobs told jurors that "[Whiting] stole the employees' money."[180] At another point, he referred to "money [Whiting] took from employees and stole"[181] and said "[Whiting] might as well have just gone into their lockers, gone through their wallet, and taken cash out."[182]

In these examples, Jacobs clearly mis-stated the evidence, attempted to mislead the jury as to the inferences it could draw, expressed his own personal belief as to the evidence, and attempted to divert the jury from deciding the case on the evidence. As such, he committed multiple ethics violations.[183]

And finally, during closing rebuttal, Giampietro told jurors, "[y]ou have no idea whether Mr. Whiting has a personal guarantee or might have had a personal guarantee on the loans to LaSalle."[184] This was a key area of contention during trial since the government had alleged that I had absolutely no risk in owning Badger, which allowed me to "milk" my company without any consequence.[185] However, during trial there was direct evidence admitted that I had personal guarantees on Badger loans with LaSalle Bank, thus a substantial personal risk if these loans were not repaid, a fact that directly rebutted this allegation.[186] Consequently, since Giampietro was the last to speak to the jury in his closing rebuttal, he desperately attempted to change jurors' recollection of this evidence just before they went into deliberations.

Giampietro did not limit his misconduct to misleading jurors; he also attempted to mislead another finder of fact—the Seventh Circuit Court. In his appellate brief, Giampietro told the appellate court that I did not give Palkowski permission to authorize MBA to pay any medical bills; I would only approve the payment of prescription expenses.[187] However, the government's own evidence at trial demonstrated that I had authorized and paid over $116,000 in Badger medical claims, which were substantially all *medical bill* payments.[188]

What does this say about the intent and character of this prosecutor? It tells you that he, like others, is willing to do whatever it takes, including breaking laws, violating ethics rules, and deliberately violating constitutional rights to due process—in order to win his case.[189] But of course in doing so he knew he was protected by absolute immunity and that his employer, the Department of Justice, had never fired any of its prosecutors or won a criminal case against any of them.

I hope this chapter has helped to shed light on how you will likely fare if you ever have the misfortune to become the prey of a federal prosecutor. The answer is: not very well. Regardless if you are innocent or not, prosecutors know their advantages and will exploit them to put you in prison. If you are innocent, the only chance you have is to make sure your attorney scrutinizes every move the government makes to be sure your rights are protected and that you receive a fair and legal trial.

Chapter 23

Case Studies of Prosecutorial Abuse

THERE ARE MANY CASES demonstrating how overzealous and shady federal prosecutors trample on the rights of U.S. citizens. But I believe there are many more cases that don't get exposed. The victimized defendants in these cases are scared to death and just want to serve their time and move on with their lives. However, I would like to present a few notable cases that showcase prosecutorial misconduct at its worst.

Axion Corp.

The case of Alex Latifi illustrates just how a rogue federal prosecutor can conduct an out-of-control and reckless prosecution of an innocent man. Federal prosecutors alleged that Latifi, owner of Axion Corp., a military parts supplier in Huntsville, Alabama, violated U.S. export laws by sending to China classified drawings of an Army Black Hawk helicopter part and falsifying related tests. In 2006, the government froze $2.5 million in company assets. Then, in March 2007, U.S. Attorney Alice Martin unsealed a multi-count criminal indictment against Latifi. Kenneth Wainstein, assistant attorney general for national security, stated that "[k]eeping sensitive U.S. military technology from falling into the wrong hands is a top priority for the Justice Department," and "[t]his indictment and other recent illegal export prosecutions should serve as a warning to companies seeking to enhance their profits at the expense of Americans' national security."

During a seven-day trial in the fall of 2007, the government's case quickly unraveled. The informant who had tipped off investigators to Latifi's alleged illegal activities turned out to be an Axion employee who was simultaneously embezzling company funds. Prosecutors also conceded that they had failed to mark the sensitive technical drawing that Latifi was accused of allegedly exporting with the warning language Defense Department regulations require. U.S. District Court Judge Inge Johnson called the government's case "sloppy" before swiftly dismissing all charges.[190]

Fischer Homes

Another horror story involves one of the country's largest home builders, Fischer Homes, based in Crestview Hills, Kentucky. The following is the text of a highly relevant *Washington Post* article by Jon Entine, published on July 21, 2009, that tells this story and proves my point about how federal prosecutors recklessly prosecute innocent business people.

> Three years ago, with TV crews rolling, police helicopters swooped down on construction sites in northern Kentucky overseen by Fischer Homes, one of the nation's one hundred largest home builders. SWAT teams arrested seventy-six Hispanic-looking workers. Armed agents handcuffed and shackled four

Fischer superintendents at their homes. Government investigators then locked down the company's headquarters and carted off thousands of documents while workers were held in conference rooms, forbidden even to contact their families. "We don't randomly pick companies. We follow evidence and go where it leads," said a spokesman for Homeland Security's Immigration and Customs Enforcement, which helped arrange for the raids to be broadcast.

It was the beginning of a three-year nightmare for Fischer Homes that concluded with its exoneration—making it a case study in the dangers of politicized prosecution: What are the consequence when the wheels of justice begin to grind, assuming a logic that sometimes precludes reason and fairness.

The raid came as the immigration debate was once again playing out in Congress. Media reports, stoked by government news releases, portrayed Fischer Homes as a greedy corporation cheating Americans out of jobs. Seven Fischer associates were eventually charged with harboring illegal immigrants. Each faced fines of up to $250,000 and as many as ten years in jail. The company was threatened with a felony indictment, including charges of money laundering, under the racketeering laws designed to target organized criminals; conviction would have ruined the company and cost the jobs of almost 500 associates and thousands more subcontracted workers. With a figurative gun at his head, founder Henry Fischer was offered a deal: Plead guilty to a felony, pay a $1 million fine and your employees will be off the hook.[191]

Mr. Fischer refused to take a plea and started preparing to go to trial. As it turned out, the government's case started to unravel and all charges were eventually dropped. Fischer Homes remains in business to this day. Incredibly but not surprisingly, the prosecutor was never punished.[192]

The problem was that the prosecutor's facts were wrong—Fischer had no undocumented workers on its payroll and the documents confiscated in the raid showed that the company's adherence to immigration and civil rights statutes, which limit what an employer can do even if it suspects its subcontractors have hired illegal immigrants, was exemplary. But the justice system wields enormous power, which often depends on extracting plea deals, sometimes from the innocent and often from supposedly deep-pocketed businesses and business owners.

As the government's case against Fischer Homes and its associates disintegrated, prosecutors increased pressure on indicted employees to agree to a plea deal—to perjure themselves—in return for the charges being dropped. Remarkably, they refused.

Despite facing humiliation and possible financial ruin, Fischer gambled his company, spending far more than the $1 million fine the government offered to fight this unjustified and unwarranted case. "I just couldn't bring myself to write that check when we did nothing wrong," Henry Fischer said.[193]

Charles Farinella

In May 2003, Charles Farinella bought 1.6 million bottles of Henri's Salad Dressing from ACH Foods. The label on each bottle said "best when purchased by" and provided a month and a year between January and June 2003. Farinella resold the salad dressing to dollar stores but before shipping, changed the dates to around July 2004 by pasting new labels over the old ones. The government argued that the "best when purchased by" date was the date on which the dressing would "expire."

Farinella was indicted and convicted by a jury of wire fraud (18 U.S.C. § 1343) and of introducing into interstate commerce a misbranded food with intent to defraud or mislead (21 U.S.C. §§ 331[a], 333[a][2]). The judge sentenced him to five years' probation (including six months of home confinement) and to pay a $75,000 fine and forfeit the net gain from the offense, which was in excess of $400,000.[194]

Farinella appealed his conviction. His appeal mainly argued that there was insufficient admissible evidence to convict him of misbranding. The government's cross-appeal challenged the sentence as too lenient. *The Seventh Circuit Court of Appeals immediately reversed his conviction.*[195]

According to the appeals court, the term "expiration date" on a food product, unlike a "best when purchased by" date, has a generally understood meaning: it is the date after which you shouldn't eat the product. Salad dressing, however, or at least the type of salad dressing represented by Henri's, is what is called "shelf stable": it has no expiration date. There is no suggestion that selling salad dressing after the "best when purchased by" date endangers human health; so far as appears, Henri's Salad Dressing is edible a decade or more after it is manufactured. There is no evidence that the taste of any of the 1.6 million bottles of Henri's Salad Dressing sold by the defendant had deteriorated by the time of trial—four years after the latest original "best when purchased by" date—let alone by the latest relabeled "best when purchased by" date, which was eighteen months after the original "best when purchased by" date. There is no evidence that any buyer of any of the 1.6 million bottles sold by the defendant ever complained about the taste.[196]

At trial, the government presented no evidence that "best when purchased by" has a uniform meaning in the food industry. In mid-trial, the government was allowed to call as an expert witness an employee of the Food and Drug Administration. He testified that the FDA has a database of inquiries regarding the relabeling of food product, that he had looked in the database, and that he had found no record of an inquiry from the defendant concerning the relabeling of salad dressing. The suggestion was that changing the "best when purchased by" date on a label requires the FDA's permission.

As stated in the appellate decision, the government's own statements were "false and misleading"—in her opening argument the principal prosecutor said that "it's a case about taking nearly two million bottles of old, expired salad dressing and relabeling it with new expiration dates to pass it off as new and fresh . . . [N]obody wants to eat foul, rancid food." During closing arguments the prosecutor told jurors, "don't let the defendant and his high-paid lawyer buy his way out of this."[197]

The Prosecution of Georgia Thompson

The government's conduct here in my opinion is so deplorable, I thought it necessary to cover the story in more detail. In 2005, Georgia Thompson was on a panel considering competitive bids for a State of Wisconsin travel contract worth up to $250,000 annually over three years. The contract was awarded to Adelman Travel, whose bid was lower than that of the other finalist, Omega Travel of Virginia, although Omega's bid scored higher on a points-based formula used by the department. It emerged that during the 2006 reelection campaign of Wisconsin Democratic governor Jim Doyle, the Adelman executives, including owner Craig Adelman, had each contributed $10,000 to the Doyle campaign, even though in previous years, including Doyle's first gubernatorial campaign, they had never given more than $1,000.[198]

In January 2006, Thompson was indicted in the U.S. Eastern District of Wisconsin on charges that she allegedly steered the contract to Adelman Travel as a reward for its campaign contributions. According to the indictment, Thompson "intentionally inflated her scores for Adelman and suggested that the other committee members do the same." After Omega still came out ahead, the indictment said Thompson convinced the panel to do a "best and final" bid round between just the two companies, which Adelman won.[199] Thompson was indicted on two felony counts: misappropriation of funds and fraud. Later that month, Governor Jim Doyle cancelled the Adelman contract but did not return the contributions.[200]

In June 2006, Thompson's jury trial started in the Wisconsin courtroom of U.S. District Judge Rudolph T. Randa. U.S. Attorney Steven Biskupic represented the government. At the end of trial, Thompson was convicted of both felony counts, and although Thompson faced a maximum twenty years in federal prison, she was sentenced by U.S. District Judge Randa to eighteen months. Shortly thereafter, Thompson reported to federal prison in Perkins, Illinois, to start her sentence.

Thompson's attorney filed an appeal with the Seventh Circuit Court. In a stunning reversal, during the April 5, 2007 oral arguments, a panel of appellate judges immediately reversed Thompson's conviction. Without waiting until completion of a written decision, the judges ordered that Thompson be released from federal prison immediately without delay. Appellate Judge Diane Woods called the prosecution's evidence "beyond thin." The court of appeals issued its written opinion in *United States v. Thompson* on April 20, 2007.

According to her attorney, the prosecution and conviction cost Thompson over $300,000, including lost pay, her savings, her condo, and her pension, which she cashed in to pay for her legal defense.

This case again demonstrates how federal prosecutors are able to use juries to convict and imprison innocent citizens for crimes which they did not commit. Another interesting detail was that the U.S. Attorney's Office and the judge in this case were the same as in my prosecution. Thompson has since been reemployed with the State of Wisconsin and as of March 5, 2008, both houses of this Wisconsin state legislature voted without dissent to reimburse Thompson $228,792 in legal expenses.

The Case of Senator Ted Stevens

Ted Stevens was a U.S. senator from the state of Alaska who, in 2008, was indicted and convicted of several federal crimes. However, before he was sentenced, the indictment and conviction was dismissed when a Department of Justice probe found evidence of serious and flagrant prosecutorial misconduct. A few years later, Stevens died in an Alaska plane crash.

Recently though, court-appointed investigator Henry Schuelke completed a review of the Stevens prosecution that had been ordered by Federal District Court Judge Emmett G. Sullivan. This report found that the prosecution "was 'permeated' by prosecutors' 'serious, widespread and at times intentional' illegal concealment of evidence that would have helped Mr. Stevens defend himself at this 2008 trial."[201] Furthermore, this report recommended that *none* of the prosecutors involved in the case, who remain on the Justice Department's payroll, be prosecuted.

Let this be a lesson to all the federal prosecutors who choose to intentionally trample on the constitutional rights of U.S. citizens: Don't worry, nothing will happen to you.

These are just a few of the perhaps hundreds of cases in which federal prosecutors have abused their position in seeking to convict the innocent. Millions of dollars in taxpayer funds have been wasted and countless lives severely damaged if not destroyed at the hands of these dishonest prosecutors. Something must be done to both enforce the rule of law and protect the innocent from the ways of these ruthless people.

Chapter 24

The Need for Reform

THE NEED FOR TRUE REFORM of federal prosecutorial misconduct has never been greater. In response to *USA Today*'s 2010 series of newspaper articles exposing massive misconduct committed by federal prosecutors, the Department of Justice under Attorney General Eric Holder has created a new internal watchdog office.[202] It remains to be seen whether the DOJ under Holder's leadership is really serious about cleaning up prosecutorial misconduct and holding prosecutors accountable.

Indeed, the Department of Justice already had in place an agency called the Office of Professional Responsibility (OPR) that was created in 1975 to maintain standards of ethical and legal conduct inside their department. However, department records show that the OPR's internal investigations generally find that federal prosecutors simply "made a mistake" even after federal judges who presided over their respective trials ruled that there was substantial and serious misconduct.[203]

Moreover, prosecutors who commit flagrant misconduct are only reprimanded or suspended or enter into agreements with the Justice Department that allow them to "leave the government with reputations intact and their records unblemished."[204] Federal prosecutors have little to fear when they commit flagrant misconduct!

The citizens of the United States need Congress to enact stiff criminal laws and penalties resulting in federal prosecutors going to prison when they engage in severe misconduct that violates a person's civil rights. In comparison, the Department of Justice routinely seeks indictments against police officers for civil rights violations who end up convicted and sent to prison. To date, however, only one federal prosecutor has been criminally prosecuted for allegedly obstructing justice, and he was eventually acquitted.[205]

It's about time laws and regulations are passed to develop an independent federal agency—not one that is part of the Department of Justice—that can properly investigate federal prosecutors who violate individual's civil rights in an effort to win their case at all costs. Until then, I fear this continued and pervasive misconduct by our federal prosecutors will continue.

The Hyde Amendment

The Hyde Amendment, codified under 18 U.S.C. § 3006A, was introduced by *Representative Henry Hyde* (a Republican of Illinois) and passed into law in 1997, despite intense opposition from the Justice Department. The intent of this law was to allow federal courts to award attorney's fees and other court costs to criminal defendants when the court finds that a prosecution was vexatious, frivolous, or in bad faith.

However, it's not always easy to win such an award against the government. Under the Hyde Amendment it is an acquitted defendant's responsibility to prove that the prosecutor acted in bad faith or the case was frivolous and the claim must be filed within thirty days after the acquittal or dismissal of a criminal case.

The Aisenberg case is an example of the Hyde Amendment in action. Steven and Marlene Aisenberg's five-month-old daughter vanished from their home in Valrico, Florida. After the parents were interviewed by law enforcement, they decided to hire an attorney and perhaps due to advice of counsel, refused to cooperate with the police any further. Federal prosecutors continued to investigate and ended up building a case against the Aisenberg's based on information gained from several wiretaps placed on their phones. The little girl was never found. The indictment that was finally brought against the Aisenbergs alleged that they admitted to obstructing justice and were responsible for the death of their daughter. Eventually, the government dropped the charges for lack of evidence. The couple's attorney, Barry Cohen, sued the government for malicious prosecution and for reimbursement of their legal fees under the Hyde Amendment and won. In February 2003, the Aisenbergs were awarded $2.9 million to pay the legal fees they incurred during their five-year-long case. The district court judge who presided over the case wrote a long decision that was highly critical of the government's conduct. Furthermore, the judge ordered the government to release the grand jury transcripts to the public, saying "the public is entitled to know" about the "misdirected and overzealous prosecutorial exertions" in this case.[206]

The Citizens Protection Act

In 1992, Joseph M. McDade, a fifteen-term congressman from Pennsylvania, was indicted on five federal counts relating to bribery. He was charged with the federal crime of racketeering and conspiracy after allegedly accepting gifts and trips in exchange for diverting government contracts to a specific group of businessmen. One of the main accusations against McDade, who was the highest-ranking Republican on the House Appropriations Committee, was that in 1983 he accepted illegal campaign contributions from employees of United Chem-Con Corporation in exchange for government contracts.[207]

According to McDade, the prosecutors intimidated his friends, family, and staff and sought to damage his reputation through press leaks and other means. McDade said that federal investigators "harassed" and "hounded" him for more than three years and turned his life into "a living nightmare."[208] Denying any wrongdoing, McDade proceeded to trial. In 1996, after eight years and hundreds of thousands of dollars in legal fees, he was acquitted on all counts by a federal jury. He retired in 1998 after thirty-six years in Congress.

Outraged by his experience, before his retirement, McDade and his colleague John Murtha, a Democratic and fellow member of the Pennsylvania congressional delegation, introduced a bill called the Citizens Protection Act of 1998 to establish standards of conduct for DOJ employees and a review board to monitor compliance. Prior to 1998, federal prosecutors could be sanctioned for misconduct only by the federal courts in which they practiced or by the DOJ, their employer. However, many critics including federal judges questioned the DOJ's ability to police its own attorneys.

The Schiller Institute, which has close ties to the political activist and frequent presidential candidate Lyndon H. LaRouche, Jr., lobbied hard for the passage of this bill and insisted that a case involving LaRouche (*U.S. v. LaRouche*, 896 F.2d 815 (4th Cir. 1990)), be the center of the congressional hearing on the matter. LaRouche, along with twelve of his associates, was indicted in 1988 on charges relating to credit card fraud and obstruction of justice and was sentenced to fifteen years of imprisonment, of which he served six years. He was released from prison in 1994. During his many years of appeals, LaRouche's attorneys had alleged that the government was involved in "deliberate and systematic misconduct and abuse of power."[209]

The prosecution of LaRouche exhibited nearly every aspect of prosecutorial misconduct that the Citizens Protection Act of 1998 covers, including intentionally mis-stating evidence, withholding exculpatory evidence, and misleading the court. The support of the bill by the institute drew considerable hostility from the DOJ and its advocates. Furthermore, the National Association of U.S. Attorneys lobbied against it. Attorney General Janet Reno condemned the bill and said she would advise President Clinton to veto it should it pass Congress. (It's worth noting that Clinton himself was very much the target of politically motivated prosecutorial misconduct—first in Arkansas and then in Washington, DC, where he was relentlessly pursued by special prosecutor Kenneth Starr.)

Nevertheless, in October 1998, Congress passed HR 3396, a somewhat watered down version of the original bill. Nevertheless, this legislation curtails deliberate attempts by the DOJ to place its attorneys above the laws of ethical conduct which apply to all lawyers.

The Citizen's Protection Act has been codified at 28 U.S.C. § 530B and reads as follows:

§ 530B. Ethical standards for attorneys for the Government

a) An attorney for the Government shall be subject to State laws and rules, and local Federal court rules, governing attorneys in each State where such attorney engages in that attorney's duties, to the same extent and in the same manner as other attorneys in that State.

b) The Attorney General shall make and amend rules of the Department of Justice to assure compliance with this section.

c) As used in this section, the term "attorney for the Government" includes any attorney described in section 77.2(a) of part 77 of title 28 of the Code of Federal Regulations and also includes any independent counsel, or employee of such counsel, appointed under chapter 40.

Section 530B has been added to the Code of Federal Regulations and included in the United States Attorney's Manual.

Nevertheless, since the passage of this bill, very little if anything has been done to curtail and punish certain federal prosecutors who decide to misuse their power and trample on the constitutional rights of innocent victims who unfortunately end up in their crosshairs.

While the Hyde Amendment can be used by federal criminal defendants to attempt to recover legal fees and costs when federal government prosecutors decide to carry out frivolous and bad-faith prosecutions, and the Citizens Protection Act requires prosecutors to abide by the ethical rules in their respective states, these changes over the course of the last fourteen years have done very little to curb the continued abuses our federal prosecutors place upon the citizenry of this country.

Congress needs new laws and regulations to protect us from corrupt and overzealous federal prosecutors who decide to put their interests ahead of doing justice. Two reforms in particular need to be made: the elimination of certain absolute immunity and the establishment of an investigative agency. It is outrageous that the law provides absolute immunity to protect federal prosecutors who violate our civil rights. FBI agents and police officers are afforded "qualified immunity," which provides protection from being sued for damages unless they violate clearly established law of which a reasonable person would have known their conduct was in violation of the law. There should be a special unit separate from the Department of Justice that investigates violations by federal prosecutors and criminally prosecutes them. Then and only then will federal prosecutors think twice before using methods that violate our constitutional rights in their effort to win cases at all costs. There are far too many instances in which prosecutors flout ethics rules and trample on the constitutional right of U.S. citizens to due process.

Chapter 25

Some Advice

SINCE I TRULY BELIEVE every entrepreneur and business person is in danger of becoming the next victim of some unprincipled federal prosecutor, my first piece of advice to you is to learn how to protect yourself well before there is any indication of trouble on the horizon. I am not referring to someone who has actually committed a federal crime with criminal intent looking to escape justice. I am referring to an innocent business person who might be in the wrong place at the wrong time and could easily become the next notch in the belt of the prosecutor looking to win a case.

If you are one of the unlucky ones who gets indicted, first find the best criminal attorney you can afford. Be sure that your attorney is well versed in your type of case. If your case involves complex business transactions, be sure your lawyer has tried, and has won, cases like it.

Next, making sure your attorney actually investigates your evidence is something you need to monitor very closely. The investigator your attorney chooses is critical. Be sure it is someone who is experienced in your type of case and starts working on your case well before trial.

Lastly, you will have to make one of the most gut-wrenching decisions of your life—whether to plead out or go into battle against the U.S. government, a confrontation in which very few will prevail.

Hopefully, you'll find some useful information on these subjects in this chapter.

Cover Your Behind

Protecting yourself from the overzealous prosecutor should start well before you become the subject of a criminal investigation by federal authorities.

Generally, physical evidence such as bank records, financial statements, applications, filings, and other paper evidence, unless someone else has intentionally altered it, shows exactly what happened, what was reported, or what you placed on an application. This type of evidence, referred to as direct evidence, if discovered by defense counsel, can be used to demonstrate your innocence with federal investigators before things get out of hand and you are charged.

However, another kind of direct evidence—individual personal recollections—is a whole other matter. When individuals are interviewed by federal investigators, they must decide whether to tell the truth or lie. Their motivations to lie include a desire to cover up their own illegal conduct, their perceived wrongdoing, a belief that they need to garner favor with federal authorities so they don't turn on them, or perhaps simple dislike of you and a desire to see you hung out to dry.

Regardless of a witness's particular motivation to lie, unless there is physical evidence or another witness available to rebut his story, the only evidence available is your own statement as to what really happened; and if you are the target of the investigation, your statement will most likely not convince any government prosecutor to drop your case. So, protecting yourself before any such investigation might be started is the best prevention against the dishonest government witnesses. How can you protect yourself from a potentially dishonest witnesses? You need to define in writing your relationship, their responsibilities, and the details of any deal. Moreover, be sure that all your employees have written work rules defining their respective job responsibilities and get them to sign a document to acknowledge their acceptance of those responsibilities. Managers of departments involved with matters relating to employee benefits, disposal of waste products, payment of payroll taxes, compliance with Federal Trade Commission matters, and employment procedures should sign agreements spelling out their responsibility to comply with all laws and regulations. Also, be sure that these managers fully understand their legal requirements and are fully trained to meet the compliance standards. When federal investigators and prosecutors come around, it's all too easy for these employees to point the finger at you, the innocent business owner, when you had nothing to do with any lack of compliance.

Suppose, like me, you are the owner of a manufacturing company and you hold the position of president. You have a plant manager named John who is responsible for all of your plant's operations including the proper disposal of a particular highly toxic byproduct of your manufacturing process. The hazardous waste is picked up by a certified waste hauler at a significant cost each month. John is on a monthly bonus program to control your company's manufacturing costs. But due to rising plant costs, John has missed his monthly bonus for four months, causing him money problems and almost daily fights with his wife.

But John is creative and has a great idea. During his ride home each day, John passes a large field. He realizes that if he were to dump two or three of the drums of waste in the field each week, he could reduce plant costs enough to get the bonus. He starts doing exactly that until one day someone sees him and reports him to the authorities.

One evening, John is paid a visit from an Environmental Protection Agency (EPA) officer. During the conversation, the officer states that the EPA has been at the site where John has been dumping the hazardous waste and that they have a witness who can identify John and his vehicle as the one doing the illegal dumping. John quickly realizes the he is in serious trouble, but again John is resourceful. John tells the officer that you, his boss, instructed him to dump this hazardous waste in that field to reduce your company's costs and improve profits. John also tells the officer that you told him he would be fired unless he did what he was told.

After the meeting, the EPA officer makes a referral to the local U.S. Attorney's Office, which soon informs you that you are the now the target of a federal criminal investigation. You, of course, have no idea why. After you hire an attorney to look into this matter, you find out that you are at the center of an investigation into illegal dumping of hazardous waste and that John will be the government's key witness. During your attorney's investigation, he asks you to provide him with all the evidence that would show John was exclusively responsible for legally disposing of this hazardous waste. You provide your attorney with John's job description, which states that John was in fact accountable for properly disposing of this waste. Your attorney asks for any other evidence to show that John received this job description and that he agreed to be exclusively responsible for the proper handling of this waste. You state that you provided this job description to John during his first day on the job and that he agreed *verbally* with his responsibilities.

The government takes your case to the federal grand jury and receives their indictment. The indictment reads that you "intentionally and knowingly" ordered the disposal of hazardous waste in violation of federal criminal law. John is not indicted since he agreed to cooperate with the government and testify against you. The government offers you a plea deal which involves prison time, but you reject the offer since you did nothing wrong. Your attorney starts preparing for your criminal trial. In reviewing the government's evidence, your attorney finds a document that shows your company had a few minor EPA matters before John was hired as plant manager that resulted in a monetary fine. Your attorney advises you that you should not testify at your trial since the government will try to make you look bad by citing the fact that your company had EPA problems in the past. You reluctantly agree.

During trial, John testifies under oath that you instructed him to dump this hazardous waste in the field. John further testifies that you told him if he went along with it, he would also benefit by an increase in his monthly bonus but if he didn't, he would be immediately fired. John persuasively explains to the jury that he had no other choice but to comply with your demand since it would be difficult to find a new job in this tight job market and that he has a wife and four kids at home to feed.

Since you have owned your business for many years now and have done quite well for yourself and your family, the government admits evidence of your income, your nice home, your vacation home, your golf club membership, your expensive cars, and other personal assets that you have earned over the years. In closing, the prosecutor argues to the jury that you are a "greedy" person with all your wealth and that you just were manipulating your employee (poor John) to reduce costs at your company to line your own pockets with the benefits. Since there was nothing in evidence to rebut John's testimony, the jury believed John and the government's theory that your motive and intent for intentionally committing the crime was your desire for more profits. As a result, the jury convicts you of the alleged crime.

So how could you have protected yourself against being railroaded by the government in this case? When you initially hired John, you could have listed all of his responsibilities, including his duty to properly dispose of the hazardous waste, on your company's letterhead as a letter agreement between your company and John. You could have included a clause stating the following: "Anything contrary to these stated responsibilities herein must be in writing and signed by the parties hereto to be valid." You and John would have signed this agreement witnessed by a third party who also signed it.

This way, you would have had a document to produce during the investigation that might persuade authorities to take a pass on you and focus their attention on John. Obviously, John could still claim that you *unofficially* told him to dump the hazardous waste. But this letter, in conjunction with your testimony, would be much better for you than just your word against his. But whether you testify or not is a matter to be decided between you and your attorney.

Here is another example. You are the owner of several retail stores in your city. You have almost sixty employees and provide a 401(k) plan to which employees may contribute a part of their compensation each week. Due to the size of your organization, you have a full-time staff accountant qualified as a CPA named Susan who is responsible for weekly payroll administration, printing employees' payroll checks, paying payroll taxes, and sending 401(k) contributions deducted from employee payroll checks to the 401(k) administrator. Susan is also responsible for managing the day-to-day cash flow of your business and paying bills and vendors. You spend your time managing the stores and developing promotions to increase sales.

Unfortunately, the economy turns down and your company's sales start to suffer. Your company starts to lose money every month. Cash flow gets extremely tight, and Susan tells you that the vendor bills are getting way past due and you are getting many calls each day from creditors. You tell Susan that you believe store sales will pick up substantially in the next quarter and that business cash flow will improve. As time goes on, Susan is having a very difficult time managing the limited cash flow and finally decides to stop sending in payroll taxes and employee 401(k) contributions. She chooses instead to pay vendors who are calling her threatening to cut off supplies and/or to sue. According to Susan's rationale, once sales improve and cash flow gets better she can catch up on the unpaid payroll taxes and employee 401(k) contributions. Susan never tells you what she is doing for fear that she might be fired.

Things don't work out the way you planned, and your company's sales continue to plummet. Your business finally closes its doors. The result is that Susan has left you with more than $150,000 in unpaid payroll taxes due to the IRS and over $60,000 in unpaid employee 401(k) contributions. When you discover this, you are furious. Your employees find out that their 401(k) contributions never made it to the 401(k) administrator, and they file a complaint with the Department of Labor (DOL). A DOL investigator named Bob starts an investigation of your company.

During the process of his investigation, Bob sets up an interview with Susan. Susan is scared to death and thinks that she is in a great deal of trouble. Bob questions Susan about the sequence of events that led up to the non-payment of employee 401(k) contributions. Susan is afraid of possibly going to jail so she tells Bob that you instructed her not to pay the payroll taxes and employee 401(k) contributions since there was not enough money to go around. Bob has been with the DOL for only a year and joined the government agency as an investigator as a stepping stone to a job with the FBI's white-collar crime division. After the meeting with Susan, Bob realizes this could be a great criminal case for his career and decides to make a referral with your local U.S. Attorney's Office.

Bob meets with the Assistant U.S. Attorney (AUSA), Peter Smith, who has been assigned to your case and who is also new to the U.S. Attorney's Office, having joined right out of law school to gain trial experience. He wants to be a high-priced white-collar defense attorney someday, but the district he works in gets very few good white-collar cases. After hearing Bob's pitch about this case, AUSA Smith becomes very interested, especially because he sees a violation of both the DOL and IRS regulation and statutes. AUSA Smith decides to take the case.

During the grand jury hearing, Susan is called as a witness. AUSA Smith puts her on the stand, and she recites the same thing she told Bob—that you instructed her not to pay the payroll taxes or employee 401(k) contributions. The grand jury returns an eighteen-count indictment against you—one count for each month the taxes and 401(k) contributions were not paid. Of course, since Susan is cooperating with the government, she is not indicted.

As in the previous example, you could have protected yourself by producing a document outlining Susan's responsibilities including language that she is required to pay all outstanding payroll taxes and 401(k) contributions in accordance with laws and regulations regardless of any instruction by you to the contrary, signed by her and witnessed by a third party.

When things go bad, there are many ways for you, the owner or manager of a business, to get "railroaded" by someone else who is willing to outright lie to federal authorities in an effort in save their own skin. And many times their own actions—which they mistakenly believe are against the law—are, in fact, not criminal at all if they would only tell the truth.

As an example, using my own case, Thresa Palkowski (Badger's human resources director) innocently used the language "insurance carrier" in her meeting notice to describe Badger's new insurance plan. By telling government investigators that I instructed her to use this wording, she gave the government key evidence (although false) to concoct a story that I had planned to intentionally deceive my employees into believing that they had health insurance through an insurance company. But instead, had she just told the truth from the beginning, that she used the language "insurance carrier" as a general description of the Badger's new healthcare plan without any intent to deceive employees, I believe neither she nor I would have been charged for the alleged false statement in Count 10 of my indictment.

Be Proactive the Instant You're Targeted

There is no better time to attempt to resolve a criminal case in the federal criminal justice system than before you are indicted. And I don't mean by just going down to the U.S. Attorney's Office and agreeing to plead guilty.

So, how do you know if the government is investigating you? Normally, you will receive a "target letter" from the U.S. Attorney's Office indicating that you are the target of a criminal investigation. Otherwise, you might find out indirectly. For example, someone you know might receive a subpoena to testify in front of a grand jury proceeding or perhaps you hear that someone received a "criminal subpoena" requesting physical evidence.

Either way, once you find out that you are the subject of a criminal investigation by the U.S. Attorney's Office, immediately find yourself a competent and experienced criminal defense attorney (advice on this to follow).

Getting a prosecutor to abandon a case once considerable time and effort has been expended on it is a challenging task. Getting the prosecutor to dismiss an indictment once you are indicted will be next to impossible without some sort of a plea of guilty. Although the government is not required to share details of its investigation before you are indicted—which might leave you and your lawyer guessing as to their theory of the crime— your attorney should be discussing with you all relevant facts and events that might be the subject of the government investigation. A tip-off to the subject matter of the government's interest would be the particular government agency that is involved in the investigation.

Once you and your attorney have pinpointed the area of governmental focus, your attorney should attempt to interview possible government witnesses and hire the necessary forensic investigators to evaluate the evidence. Once equipped with this evidence, which might demonstrate flaws in the government's case, your attorney can then decide whether to use this evidence to attempt to talk the federal prosecutors out of charging you in the first place. Remember, the unscrupulous prosecutor is looking to prosecute you and put you in prison and as such win his case and advance his or her career. Evidence in the government's possession that might demonstrate your innocence is not their concern. The prosecutor is also not looking at the body of evidence in his control and custody and deciding whether you are guilty or innocent. Indeed, many times the evidence that shows your innocence is located somewhere else. If your attorney can demonstrate to the government that there is admissible evidence available that rebuts the government's theory of an alleged crime before you are indicted, your attorney stands a reasonable chance of talking the government out of seeking a grand jury indictment.

Unfortunately, in my case, my lawyer Glynn did very little, if anything, to investigate and prepare a vigorous defense before my indictment in his attempt to talk the government out of seeking any charges against me. Glynn should have investigated the issues surrounding my case at the time I hired him in July 2002, a year and a half before I was indicted. He should have met with Labor Department investigators to determine what problems they had so that we could address their issues head on.

Had Glynn done so, he would have certainly advised me to simply pay the $20,752 in Badger 401(k) contributions in July 2002 even though they were the responsibility, as a matter of law, of the purchaser of Badger's assets. He would have also determined, and would have convinced prosecutors, that the other $52,126 in employee deductions had been properly paid toward Badger's and Western's healthcare programs.

Armed with this information, Glynn would have had a very good chance of demonstrating to government authorities that no crime had been committed and that filing criminal changes against me would be frivolous and in bad faith. Glynn could have also put the government on notice that if they proceeded with charges and lost, I would be suing them for damages under the Hyde Amendment, a provision that I had discussed in the last chapter. But, of course, if Glynn had done all of that, his firm would not have collected well over $200,000 to represent me in my criminal case.

Find a Good Defense Attorney

If you find yourself on the dinner plate of a federal prosecutor who intends to make you his next meal, you will need to find the best criminal defense lawyer you can afford, right away.

If you cannot afford a private attorney, then the court will appoint you a public defender. There are many excellent public defenders but also plenty of poor ones. If you don't think your appointed attorney is properly representing you, you can ask the court to appoint you a different one.

If you have the money, find an attorney who represents white-collar clients like you most of the time. Someone who represents defendants charged with murder, rape, and armed robberies will not be right attorney for you. Also, make sure your attorney does mostly, if not exclusively, federal rather than state criminal work. The federal court system is substantially different from that of the state. I know of one individual who hired an extremely experienced criminal lawyer who had handled over two thousand criminal cases only to find out on the day of his trial that this was his first criminal case in a federal court. Not surprisingly, things did not go very well for him.

Also, be sure the attorney you select actually goes to trial with some of his clients rather than pleading them all out. You don't want a "dump truck" lawyer. You want your attorney to be an experienced and proficient trial lawyer who is routinely involved in federal trials as defense counsel.

Lastly, find an attorney who has the time to start investigating your case as soon as possible and prepare for trial. This is somewhat tricky since the best lawyers are in high demand and, as a result, are extremely busy; thus, the attorney who can start on your case right away perhaps is not the most experienced. However, beware of the lawyer who sits on your case—perhaps thinking you will eventually break down and plead out—and requests several continuances of your trial date.

Where do you find the best criminal lawyers? You might ask for a referral from an attorney you know or have worked with previously. You could sit though some federal criminal trials and observe different criminal defense lawyers in action. You could consult an online directory of criminal attorneys such as Martindale.com. Or you could find the directory *The Best Lawyers in America* at your local library.

Get Your Hands on the Evidence

In a federal criminal matter, before or after an indictment, you are not permitted to conduct a sworn deposition on any witness or conduct any other discovery method of witnesses like you can in a federal or state civil matter. Your attorney can certainly interview a government witness, if they are willing to talk to him or her, but you can't get their testimony under oath.

However, there is one way you *can* get their testimony under oath. Commence a "meritorious lawsuit" against the government's witnesses. This will allow you to get their depositions—possibly before their grand jury testimony, but if not then certainly before trial. The foundation of a meritorious case is negligence or fault of a party that causes injury or damages to you. This way, if they later cave in to the government's witness-coaching tactics, you have their sworn testimony beforehand that you can perhaps use to impeach them at a later date. But, you can't just sue them because they testified against you at a grand jury or at trial. I learned about this strategy a little bit too late. Let me explain.

One of the main issues in contention during my trial regarding the unpaid 401(k) contributions from Badger employees was who was responsible for paying them—Ron Bussan, who was Badger's controller, or myself.

I had thought the evidence was pretty clear and straightforward concerning this matter, since up to the point at which Badger's 401(k) contributions stopped getting paid, Bussan had been sending in the payroll data to Strong Funds for audit; Bussan had been receiving the 401(k) contributions due in the form of an invoice from Strong; and Bussan had been making the 401(k) payments to Strong for many months if not years. However, during trial, Bussan testified that I was the one who determined which checks were sent out and that I specifically told him not to pay the Badger employees' 401(k) contributions because "there was not enough money to go around."[210] Surprisingly, this testimony by Bussan at trial was never corroborated with any other evidence.

However, in Bussan's sworn deposition testimony, conducted after my trial, Bussan testified that he had been the one who determined which Badger checks were sent out based on "the amount of cash available."[211] He also testified that he had decided which checks would ultimately clear Badger's bank account based on "critical vendors [that] would keep [Badger] going longer."[212] If I'd had Bussan's deposition testimony before trial rather than after, assuming we could get it admitted, my attorney could have effectively used it to impeach Bussan's testimony at trial showing the jury that he was not telling the truth. My civil lawsuit against Bussan would have alleged that it was Bussan, not I, who had failed to pay over the Badger employee 401(k) contributions, and I would have had the evidence of his deposition and other documentary evidence as proof.

Another one of the government's key witnesses in my case was Thresa Palkowski. I can only imagine the tremendous pressure Palkowski was under to adapt to the government's theory of their case against me. As a result, Palkowski testified that I instructed her to use the language health insurance "carrier" rather than "administrator," which she allegedly intended to use in the meeting notice that was posted to notify Badger employees of the change in Badger's group health insurance plan.[213] Palkowski's testimony during my trial, which was uncorroborated by any other evidence, led to my conviction on Count 10 of my indictment.

Nevertheless, she told a completely different story in her sworn deposition testimony just a few weeks after my trial relating to the case I filed against Randy Lubben and LaSalle Bank. I could not use her testimony in my appeal since the appeal only deals with evidence admitted at trial.

In her deposition, Palkowski testified that:

- *she* came up with the language that was in the meeting notice;[214]

- she did not recall at whose direction the term "health insurance carrier" was added;[215]

- she did not remember me having any role in the selection of the language used in the meeting notice.[216]

Again, if I'd had Palkowski's deposition testimony before trial, my attorney could have effectively used it to impeach her trial testimony showing the jury that she was also not telling the truth.

The point here is that if you can either directly file a lawsuit against or perhaps depose any of the government's witnesses in a civil matter, this will most likely be your only chance to get their truthful testimony before federal prosecutors and their investigators get the chance to persuade these witnesses to see their case their way.

To Plead or Not to Plead, That Is the Question

Despite the fact that our federal criminal laws are draconian in nature and the prison sentences for most white-collar crimes are far too harsh, I fervently believe in the rule of law and the need for consequences if an individual knowingly and intentionally breaks the law. I would argue that if you committed a federal crime with intent, you will be best served by not going to trial and cutting the best deal you can in a plea agreement with government prosecutors.

That being said, if you *did not* commit a crime, then I believe that you should vigorously fight to prove your innocence—but understand that *you will be doing so at your own peril.* Hundreds if not thousands of innocent people choose to plead out each year rather than fight the government in order to eliminate the risk of paying a substantially higher price—both in prison and money—if they were to lose at trial. The decision is ultimately yours. As one criminal lawyer told me, the big question is not whether you are guilty or innocent but rather if the government can prove its case against you and win a conviction or not.

In any event, I was willing to go to prison for potentially a much longer time rather than stand before the court and say that I committed a crime (which will be required if you plead out) when I did not, thus committing the crime of perjury. It was a matter of principle for me, and my integrity was more important than anything else.

What if you choose to plead out rather than fight the government? First, get a good criminal lawyer. Then, assuming you have already entered a plea of not guilty, don't change your plea without a written contractual agreement between you and the government. Otherwise, you will not have the government's concessions spelled out in writing in a legally enforceable agreement for your cooperation.

Next, although your attorney perhaps will tell you otherwise, don't accept a plea agreement whereby you change your plea from not guilty to guilty before the sentencing court hands down your sentence. Unfortunately, this occurs in ninety-nine percent of the cases. Understand that federal courts will not and do not become party to plea agreements, and the sentencing judge may or may not agree with the prosecutor's recommendation and may sentence you to a much harsher sentence than your agreement with the government calls for. Also, this type of "non-binding plea" agreement in most cases allows the government to make an argument based on "relevant conduct," which is conduct with which you were not charged. In other words, while the prosecutor is arguing out of one side of his mouth that you should be sentenced to a year and one day (because the plea agreement he signed requires him to do so), he can argue out of the other side of this mouth that you are a really bad guy for all kinds of things you were *not charged* with. The prosecutor will also throw in any criminal convictions you might have had in your past to further incite the judge.

There is perhaps a better way—and that's getting what's called a "binding plea agreement."[217] Its terms state that if the sentencing court does not accept the sentence negotiated between the defendant and the government as part of the plea agreement and ends up handing down a stiffer sentence, then you are permitted to take back your guilty plea and go to trial.

However, the government and your attorney both dislike this type of plea. The government certainly will not bring it up since it wants the case to be over with. Your attorney most likely won't bring it up because he has charged you a flat non-refundable retainer fee and wants finality to your case as soon as possible. Either way, stand your ground and insist on this type of plea agreement. You are giving up all of your rights and should receive the deal you bargained for or be permitted to go to trial.

But also consider this. The binding plea can be a double-edged sword. If you enter into this type of plea agreement, you might end up with a higher sentence than you otherwise were entitled to receive. For example, if your sentencing guideline calls for a sentence of five to six years but the judge thinks your sentence should be only three years, the judge must follow the terms of the binding plea agreement of a four-year sentence or void the agreement, take back your not-guilty plea, and schedule you for trial. Therefore, in this example, the judge would be unable to give you the three-year sentence he or she felt was appropriate.

Also, defendants who select a binding plea *may* be ineligible for any future sentence reductions that might become available. This is because over the years, several circuits have concluded that a sentence prearranged in a plea agreement is not based on a lower sentencing range. Instead, the sentence imposed in a

Rule 11(c)(1)(C) plea comes directly from the agreement itself, not from the sentencing guidelines.[218] Still, there have been appellate courts willing to show some flexibility. For example, in *U.S. v. Dews*, 551 F.3d 204 (4th Cir. 2008), the panel held that the defendants who had entered binding pleas were entitled to the benefit of sentence reductions under 18 U.S.C. § 3582(c). In other words, you need to find out your circuit's legal precedence regarding this matter before you decide the best type of plea agreement to use.

In my case, the prosecutor offered me a non-binding plea to one count in return for his arguing to the judge that my sentence should be a year and a day. My attorney agreed with his offer and suggested that I take it, but I am glad I didn't since I believe it was a setup. First, while the prosecutor would have been required to recommend to the court that I receive a sentence of a year and a day in accordance with the written plea agreement, out of the other side of his mouth he would have most likely incited the judge just as he did during my initial sentencing. This type of plea would have allowed him to do just that. Alternatively, he could have argued "relevant conduct"—meaning he could have brought up other conduct for which I was not charged, such as the healthcare claims, or charges for which I was acquitted. My only protection would have been the fact that the count for which I would have been pleading guilty had a five-year statutory maximum sentence. Therefore, I believe I would have received a five-year sentence, which was the maximum the judge could have given. And of course, this type of plea would have prohibited me from appealing anything except perhaps the voluntary nature of my plea. I would have more than likely given away my right to file a collateral attack on the conviction pursuant to 28 U.S.C. § 2255 to prove my innocence.

While this is by no means a complete list of all the things you need to be concerned about both before and after an indictment, understanding how our federal criminal justice system *really* works and the fact that all federal prosecutors are not necessarily law-abiding enforcement officials will go a long way in keeping you alert and thinking in the event that something like this happens to you.

Epilogue

I T IS NOW THE BEGINNING OF SEPTEMBER 2012 and I just received notice, after three long years, that Judge Randa denied my motion for a new trial—no surprise there. I will press on with an appeal to the Seventh Circuit Court. I originally filed my motion back in July of 2009. It took the government prosecutor, Gordon Giampietro, over a year to respond.

Unfortunately, there is no time frame within which the court must rule on my motion, and I am not sure of the reason for the court's delay. However, since this whole matter began some ten years ago when my attorney told me I was going to be indicted, I have been committed to seeking justice if that means taking my case to the Seventh Circuit Court and afterward to the Supreme Court, if they will hear my case.

The prosecutor in my case, Gordon Giampietro, is still a federal prosecutor for the Eastern District of Wisconsin. In 2007, he applied for a federal judgeship to replace Judge Randa, who had announced his retirement. Randa later changed his mind and stayed on. Randy Lubben's company, Wisconsin Die Casting (the buyer of Badger), finally closed its doors in 2008, and shortly thereafter Lubben filed for personal bankruptcy. It appears he lost everything including all the equity in his house.

If you are a business owner, you know how much risk and commitment is involved. There are many hours of hard work, uncertainty as to the economy and other factors out of your control, the need to trust in the honesty and competence of others, and there may even be some investment of personal money, which may even mean risking your entire net worth.

But I hope you now realize that there is a much larger risk to business ownership that you need to be concerned about and that is the unscrupulous and well-protected federal prosecutor. Until our laws and regulations are changed and enforced to punish those federal prosecutors who are willing to use their unprecedented power to win at all costs, we are all in danger.

In the meantime, what can we do? If there is one piece of advice I can give a business person who has become the target of a federal prosecutor, it is to hire the best attorney you can afford who has your best interest at heart. Then gather the evidence that demonstrates your innocence and get your attorney to use this evidence to talk the prosecutor out of indicting you. I am sure there will be many defense lawyers who will dispute this advice. They will say you'd be making a mistake to show your hand to the prosecutors—in other words, tipping them off to what your evidence and defense strategy will be at trial. But trust me: if you are indicted, innocent or not, chances are those hands of yours will soon be behind your back as you are carted off to a federal penitentiary. After you are indicted, your chance of success is highly unlikely since you have now entered the prosecutor's world—in which he or she holds most, if not all, the cards.

I hope that you have found my true story both compelling and informative. I also hope I have provided you with some knowledge of the workings of the federal criminal justice system and revealed just what will go on behind the scenes if, God forbid, you become a federal criminal defendant. If it turns out that you are unfortunate enough to become the target of the U.S Attorney's Office and are indicted—and are innocent of the allegations made—you and your family have a long, painful road ahead of you no matter if you plead out or go to trial. You will not come out of this unscathed either way. If this is the case, I wish you the best in the battle of your lifetime.

Endnotes

1. Confidential Acquisition Analysis for Badger Die Casting Corp. #SE-1276 Dated October 31, 1997. Published by Mertz Associates, Inc.
2. Badger Die Casting Corporation Reviewed Financial Statements ending December 31, 1998. Reviewed by Komisar, Brady & Co., LLP. Certified Public Accountants.
3. Badger Die Casting Corporation Reviewed Financial Statements ending December 31, 1999. Review by Komisar, Brady & Co., LLP. Certified Public Accountants.
4. Badger Union Contract Effective November 1, 1999 though October 31, 2002, ¶ 13.2, pp. 18–19.
5. The United Healthcare Group policy states "[United] reserves the right to change the schedule of rates for Premiums . . . at least 31 days prior to the effective date of the change." If, on the other hand, the premiums involve an increase of 25% or more then United must give notice "at least 60 days prior to the effective date of the change." (Group Number 200971, p. 9).
6. Specifically, the Union Contract required "Before making any changes, the Company will notify the Union." (¶ 13.2, p. 19).

7. Steven Chapman, MBA's Vice-President of Operations, testified that "there will be employee meetings set up . . . for employees to come in and be told of the change. Who the administrator is, and potentially if there is any plan changes, they would be notified of that." (Trial Tr., p. 103).

8. Trial Tr., 105, Gov. Ex. 7.

9. Lubben signed this Confidentially Agreement on January 25, 2002.

10. Lubben's Employment Agreement dated May 5, 1999, (§ (2)(c)).

11. http://en.wikipedia.org/wiki/NLRB.

12. Union Contact clearly spells out that Badger "reserves the right to select the insurance carrier or become self-insured," Badger Union Contract Effective 11/01/99, pp. 18–19, § 13.2.

13. Letter dated May 9, 2008 from the NLRB Regional Director Irving E. Gottschalk.

14. Order of Dismissal signed by U.S. Magistrate Judge Aaron E. Goldstein dated April 18, 2008.

15. *Steven E. Whiting v. LaSalle Bank, Randell E. Lubben, and Wisconsin Die Casting, LLC.* Case Number 02 L 013912. Circuit Court of Cook County, Illinois, filed April 9, 2004.

16. Order and Memorandum Option of the Circuit Court of Cook County, Illinois dated April 4, 2005, case number 02 L 013912.

17. *State of Wisconsin v. Badger Die Casting, et al.*, No. 04-cv-003823.

18. Ibid.

19. *Chao v. The Garrett Group, LLC, et al.*, Case No. 04-C-0849-CNC, Doc. 51, ¶¶ 11–12.

20. Bussan testified in his deposition that he notified Whiting that he had wired Badger's December 2001 401(k) fund to Strong (Bussan's 08/30/05 Depo., p. 51).

21. Email from Thomas Preusker at Strong Funds dated January 14, 2002.
22. *Upholsterers' International v. Artistic Furniture*, 920 F.2d 1323, 1329 (7th Cir.1990); *Chicago Truck Drivers v. Tasemkin, Inc.*, 59 F.3d 48, 49 (7th Cir. 1995).
23. *Chao v. The Garrett Group, LLC, et al.*, Case No. 04-C-0849-CNC, Doc. 9.
24. *Chao v. Steven Whiting, et al.*, Case No. 04-CV-599-RM, Doc. 1, ¶¶ 11–12.
25. Ibid., Doc. 28.
26. Opposition Of The United States To Defendant's Motion In Limine, Doc. 57, p. 8.
27. Trial Tr., p. 5.
28. Ibid., p. 14.
29. The Court stated: "the Government has asked that . . . it be allowed to present [wealth evidence] in its opening statements . . . to show the jury what the evidence will disclose . . . The Court will allow the Government to make that argument, in opening [a]nd if the evidence discloses it, [the Government can] make t[hat] argument subsequent." (Trial Tr., pp. 22, 23).
30. Ibid., pp. 38, 39.
31. Ibid., pp. 204–12, 535–38.
32. Ibid., pp. 758–60.
33. Ibid., pp. 762–63.
34. Ibid., pp. 763–65.
35. Ibid., p. 764.
36. Ibid., p. 768.
37. Ibid., p. 772.
38. Ibid., pp. 808–09.
39. Ibid., pp. 809–11.
40. Ibid., p. 900.
41. Ibid., p. 835.

42. *Best v. District of Columbia*, 291 U.S. 411, 54 S. Ct. 487, 78 L. Ed. 882 (1934).
43. *U.S. v. Brockington*, 849 F.2d 872, 875 (4th Cir. 1988).
44. Standard 3-5.5 Opening Statement: ABA Standards for Criminal Justice: Prosecution Function (3rd Edition).
45. Trial Tr., p. 41.
46. Ibid., p. 912.
47. Ibid., pp. 332–33.
48. Ibid., p. 333.
49. Ibid., pp. 378–80.
50. Standard 3-5.8 Argument to the Jury: ABA Standards for Criminal Justice: Prosecution Function (3rd Edition).
51. Ibid.
52. Trial Tr., p. 903.
53. Ibid., p. 835.
54. Standard 3-5.8(a), ABA Standard For Criminal Justice (3rd ed. 1993). See also, Module Rule 3.4(e); 4.1(a); 8.4(a,c,d) ABA Module Rules of Professional Conduct (5th. ed.).
55. Trial Tr., pp. 958–59.
56. Ibid., p. 244.
57. Ibid., p. 970.
58. Ibid., p. 374.
59. Ibid., pp. 956–57.
60. Ibid., pp. 373–74.
61. Ibid., p. 926.
62. Gov. Trial Ex. 97.
63. Count 1 in the indictment.
64. *Whiting v. United States of America*, 09-CV-00730, Memo, pp. 7–8.
65. Counts 5 through 9 in the indictment.
66. Ibid., pp. 14–20.
67. Count 10 in the indictment.

68. Interview Memorandum by Detective Spang—dated April 15, 2005.
69. *Whiting v. United States of America*, 09-CV-00730, Memo, pp. 35–38.
70. Counts 3 and 4 in the indictment.
71. Gov. Trial Ex. 97.
72. *Whiting v. United States of America*, 09-CV-00730, Memo, pp. 11–12.
73. Count 13 in the indictment.
74. Trial Tr., pp. 553, 671.
75. *Whiting v. United States of America*, 09-CV-00730, Memo, pp. 24–27.
76. Ibid., pp. 29–32.
77. *Chao v. The Garrett Group, LLC, et al.*, Case No. 04-C-0849-CNC, Doc. 51.
78. *Upholsterers' International v. Artistic Furniture*, 920 F.2d 1323, 1329 (7th Cir. 1990); *Chicago Truck Drivers v. Tasemkin, Inc.*, 59 F.3d 48, 49 (7th Cir. 1995).
79. *Chao v. Steven Whiting, et al.*, Case No. 04-CV-599-RM, Doc. 102.
80. Ibid., Doc. 108.
81. Gov. Trial Ex. 97.
82. Prosecutor Giampietro told the jury during his opening statements "I want to emphasize this case does not charge the Defendant with converting total dollar amount of unpaid medical claims." (Trial Tr., p. 43).
83. A defendant could technically bypass the direct appeal and file a 28 U.S.C. § 2255 Motion right way after trial but they would be giving up their direct appeal rights.
84. Jury Instructions, Doc. 69, pp. 15, 16, 21.
85. Whiting's App. Br., pp. 18–23.
86. Ibid., p. 30.

87. Ibid.
88. Ibid., pp. 31–32.
89. Ibid., pp. 33–34.
90. Ibid., pp. 44–53.
91. The United States of America Re-Sentencing Memorandum, Doc. 170-2, p. 3.
92. *Strickland v. Washington*, 466 U.S. 668, 686, (1984).
93. Ibid.
94. *Whiting v. United States of America*, 09-CV-00730, Memo, pp. 7–9.
95. Badger employees paid 15% of the total healthcare premium paid by Badger.
96. *Whiting v. United States of America*, 09-CV-00730, Memo, pp. 8–10.
97. Ibid., pp. 11–13.
98. Ibid., pp. 13–14.
99. Ibid., pp. 15–17.
100. Ibid., pp. 17–19.
101. *Chao v. The Garrett Group, LLC, et al.*, Case No. 04-C-0849-CNC, Doc. 102, 108.
102. *Whiting v. United States of America*, 09-CV-00730, Memo, pp. 20–22.
103. Ibid., pp. 22–24.
104. Ibid., pp. 35–38.
105. Ibid.
106. Ibid.
107. Ibid.
108. Ibid.
109. Trial Tr., p. 41.
110. *Whiting v. United States of America*, 09-CV-00730, Memo, pp. 24–26.
111. Ibid., pp. 26–27.
112. Ibid.

113. Opposition Of The United States To Defendant's Motion In Limine, Doc. 57, p. 8.
114. Trial Tr., p. 14.
115. Trial Tr., pp. 38–39.
116. *Whiting v. United States of America*, 09-CV-00730, Memo, pp. 29–31.
117. Ibid., pp. 31–32.
118. Trial Tr., p. 900.
119. *Whiting v. United States of America*, 09-CV-00730, Memo, pp. 32–33.
120. Data compiled from Badger's Balance Sheet and Profit & Loss Statements.
121. *Whiting v. United States of America*, 09-CV-00730, Doc. 1.
122. Ibid., Doc. 5.
123. Gov. App. Br., Doc. 9.
124. Ibid., Doc. 9, p. 15.
125. Ibid., Fitzgerald Aff. ¶ 13.
126. Ibid., Fitzgerald Aff. ¶ 7.
127. Ibid., Fitzgerald Aff. ¶ 8.
128. Ibid., Fitzgerald Aff. ¶ 9.
129. Whiting's Reply Br., Doc. 12.
130. Whiting's Reply Br., Doc. 12, pp. 2–3.
131. Model Rule of Professional Conduct, 3.8(g)(2)(ii).
132. *Green v. U.S.*, 356 U.S. 165 (1958).
133. http://www.truthinjustice.org/grandjury.htm.
134. http://www.nacdl.org/grandjury/.
135. http://www.nacdl.org/criminaldefense.aspx?id=10372&terms =grand+jury+bill+of+rights.
136. Ibid.
137. http://articles.philly.com/1996-02-02/news/25655377_1_ grand-jurors-grand-jury-doughnuts.
138. *United States v. Williams*, 504 U.S. 36, 38 (1992).
139. *United States v. Isgro*, 974 F.2d 1091 (9th Cir. 1992).

140. *United States v. DiBernardo*, 552 F.Supp. 1315 (S.D. Fla. 1982).
141. ABA Standard for Criminal Justice: Prosecution Function (Standard 3-3.6(b), 3rd ed.).
142. http://www.post-gazette.com/win/justice.asp.
143. http://www.usatoday.com/news/washington/judicial/2010-09-22-federal-prosecutors-reform_N.htm.
144. http://www.poynter.org/latest-news/mediawire/128831/sidney-hillman-foundation-announces-2011-prize-winners/.
145. http://www.justice.gov/opa/documents/pmru-creation.pdf.
146. *Imbler v. Pachtman*, 96 S.Ct. 982 (1976).
147. Ibid., 425–26 (1976).
148. Ibid., 426–29 (1976).
149. "Swearing the oath to presumed innocence" (HoustonChroncle.com, January 15, 2006).
150. Ibid.
151. Trial Tr., p. 997.
152. *U.S. v. Skilling*, Crim. No. H-04-25, Decl. of Edward J. Bronson §15.
153. Ibid.
154. *In Re Winship*, 397 U.S. at 363–64.
155. Dorothy K. Kagehiro: Defining the Standard of Proof in Jury Instructions, at 196–97.
156. http://www.ca7.uscourts.gov/pjury.pdf.
157. U.S. Sentencing Commission, 2010 Datafiles, USSCFY10.
158. Ibid.
159. This is the flapcopy from the book "Three Felonies a Day: How the Feds Target the Innocent" by Harvey A. Silverglate.
160. *Dixon v. United States*, 126 S. Ct. 2437, 2441 (2006).
161. *Bryan v. United States*, 524 U.S. 184, 192 (1998).
162. Ibid., at 192.
163. *Brady v. Maryland*, 373 U.S. 83 (1963).

164. http://www.mainjustice.com/justanticorruption/2011/12/01/
     judges-sending-clear-message-against-prosecutor-tactics-
     defense-lawyers-argue/.
165. http://www.justicedenied.org/master.htm.
166. http://moritzlaw.osu.edu/osjcl/Articles/Volume7_2/Freedman-
     FinalPDF.pdf.
167. ABA Standard for Criminal Justice: Prosecution Function
     (Standard 3-5.5, cmt. 3rd ed.).
168. Trial Tr., p. 41.
169. *Whiting v. United States of America*, 09-CV-00730, Memo,
     pp. 24–26.
170. ABA Standard for Criminal Justice: Prosecution Function
     (Standard 3-5.5, 3rd ed.).
171. Ibid., Standard 3-5.8(a), 3rd ed.
172. Ibid., Standard 3-5.8(b-d), 3rd ed.
173. *Berger v. United States*, 295 U.S. 78, 85 (1935).
174. *United States v. Berger*, 73 F.2d 278 (1934).
175. Trial Tr., pp. 379–81.
176. Ibid., p. 909.
177. ABA Standard for Criminal Justice: Prosecution Function
     (Standard 3-5.8(cmt), 3rd ed.).
178. Trial Tr., p. 903.
179. Ibid., p. 835.
180. Ibid., p. 901.
181. Ibid., p. 902.
182. Ibid., p. 913.
183. ABA Standard for Criminal Justice: Prosecution Function
     (Standard 3-5.8(a-d), 3rd ed.).
184. Trial Tr., pp. 958–59.
185. Ibid., pp. 918–19, 900.
186. Ibid., p. 244.
187. Gov. App. Br., p. 11.

188. Gov. Trial Exh. 101.
189. ABA Standard for Criminal Justice: Prosecution Function (Standard 3-5.8(a-d), 3rd ed.).
190. http://www.abajournal.com/magazine/article/the_curious_case_of_alex_latifi/.
191. http://www.washingtonpost.com/wp-dyn/content/article/2009/07/20/AR2009072002355_pf.html.
192. The book: No Crime But Prejudice by Jon Entine.
193. http://www.aei.org/article/a-parable-of-politicized-prosecution/.
194. http://www.mwe.com/info/news/farinella.pdf.
195. Ibid.
196. Ibid.
197. *United States v. Farinella*, 558 F. 3d 695 (7th Cir. 2009).
198. "Agency disputes travel bids" Milwaukee Journal Sentinel (October 19, 2005).
199. "State official indicted in travel contract case" Milwaukee Journal Sentinel (January 24, 2006).
200. "Doyle kills travel deal" Milwaukee Journal Sentinel (January 31, 2006).
201. http://www.nytimes.com/2011/11/22/us/politics/no-charges-recommended-against-prosecutors-in-ted-stevens-case.html.
202. http://www.usatoday.com/news/washington/judicial/2011-01-18-prosecutors_N.htm.
203. http://www.usatoday.com/news/washington/judicial/2010-09-22-federal-prosecutors-reform_N.htm.
204. http://www.usatoday.com/news/washington/judicial/2010-12-08-prosecutor_N.htm?csp=hf.
205. http://www.winston.com/index.cfm?contentID=154&itemID=3733.
206. http://www.fedcrimlaw.com/visitors/punchltd/2003/05-05-03.html#Aisenberg.

207. *United States of America v. Joseph M. McDade*, 28 F.3d 283 (3rd Cir. 1994).
208. http://www.nytimes.com/1992/05/06/us/top-republican-on-a-house-panel-is-charged-with-accepting-bribes.html?scp=1&sq=McDade&st=nyt.
209. http://en.wikipedia.org/wiki/Lyndon_LaRouche.
210. Trial Tr., p. 243.
211. Bussan's Deposition dated 08/30/05, p. 22.
212. Ibid., p. 26.
213. Trial Tr., p. 332.
214. Thresa Palkowski's Deposition dated 08/30/05, p. 29.
215. Ibid., p. 30.
216. Ibid., p. 31.
217. Fed.R.Crim.P., 11(c)(1)(C).
218. *U.S. v. Cieslowski*, 410 F.3d 353, 364 (7th Cir. 2005).

About the Author

STEVEN E. WHITING has been an entrepreneur, consultant, business owner and advisor for the past thirty years. He has consulted to over 200 small companies on matters relating to restructuring and revitalizing of distressed businesses. He has also owned and operated over fifteen companies in a variety of industries.

Index

Made in the USA
Lexington, KY
18 June 2013